Eye-Witness
HIROSHIMA

Edited by
ADRIAN WEALE

Robinson
LONDON

Robinson Publishing Ltd
7 Kensington Church Court
London W8 4SP

First published in the UK by
Robinson Publishing Ltd 1995

A copy of the British Library Cataloguing in Publication
data is available from the British Library

ISBN 1–85487–392–X

Printed and bound in the EC

10 9 8 7 6 5 4 3 2 1

Contents

Acknowledgements

It would not have been possible to have written this book without the extremely generous assistance, advice and encouragement of my father, Ken Weale (otherwise known as Dr K. E. Weale Ph.D DIC FIC). He made sure that I understood what I was writing about and drew my attention to a great many things that he correctly felt I should be writing about. In addition, his lucid and easily understood explanation of the evolution of atomic theory survives virtually unchanged in the first section of the book.

I would also like to thank the staffs of the Public Records Office at Kew; the Imperial War Museum Department of Printed Books; the Haldane Library of the Imperial College of Science, Technology and Medicine; Kensington Public Library; and Chiswick Public Library. I am very grateful for their courteous assistance.

Mark Crean and everyone at Robinson's have shown remarkable tolerance as I struggled to get the manuscript finished in time to fit in with their schedules – sorry, folks! And I must, as always, thank my agent Andrew Lownie for his enthusiasm, encouragement and ability.

Finally, I would also like to thank my wife Mary and my son Robert for putting up with me whilst I finished the book.

Introduction

In the second week of January 1939, the Danish physicist Niels Bohr was travelling from Europe to the United States aboard the Swedish liner *Drottningholm*. The nine-day voyage was rough and Bohr was frequently sea-sick but, even so, he forced himself to concentrate on some fascinating information that had just been imparted to him by a young Jewish refugee from Nazi Germany called Otto Frisch. Frisch had just spent the Christmas and New Year holidays with his aunt, another refugee scientist called Lise Meitner, in Sweden, and together they had spent some time pondering the strange experimental results that had been achieved by Meitner's former research partner, the German chemist Otto Hahn, at the Kaiser Wilhelm Institute in the Berlin suburb of Dahlem.

Hahn had been experimentally bombarding uranium atoms with neutrons in an effort to create what are called '*transuranic*' elements – that is, elements beyond uranium in the periodic table, which do not exist naturally on earth – but his tests seemed to show that the actual products of this bombardment were the two known elements barium and lanthanum. This result seemed contrary to any sensible theory that Hahn was aware of and he wanted Meitner's advice as a long-standing friend and confidante; and as a brilliant scientist.

The solution worked out by Meitner and Frisch, which so excited Niels Bohr as he sailed to New York, was that the nuclei of the uranium atoms under bombardment were in fact breaking into two similar-sized smaller nuclei – barium and lanthanum nuclei in fact – and emitting a little burst of energy as they did so. It was an explanation that was crucial to our understanding of the structure of the atomic nucleus and was intensely exciting to the physicists of the late 1930s, who were finally beginning to unravel the mysteries of the fundamental nature of matter. Niels Bohr was the father figure of nuclear physics at that time – a man with a host of outstanding achievements to his name – and this splitting of the atomic nucleus confirmed a theory that Bohr had developed likening the nucleus to a liquid drop.

On arrival in America one of Bohr's travelling companions accidentally leaked the news to the US scientific community, and Bohr decided, to protect Meitner and Frisch's 'claim' on the discovery, that he would announce it at a conference he was attending in Washington, giving full credit to Hahn and his colleague Fritz Strassman, who had performed the original experiment, and to Meitner and Frisch, who had so brilliantly interpreted the results. Thus it was that the world came to hear about 'nuclear fission', as Frisch had named the process.

Although nuclear fission was clearly of great import to those with an interest in scientific matters, it is not immediately apparent how it came to impinge on the rest of the world. The answer is in the little burst of energy released as the atomic nucleus splits in two. Frisch made the calculation that the energy released by one uranium atom splitting would be enough to make a visible grain of sand jump in the air. But atoms are very small, even in comparison to grains of sand: a German physicist, Siegfried Flugge, shortly afterwards calculated that the energy release caused by the fission of all the atoms in a cubic metre of uranium oxide would actually be sufficient to raise a cubic kilometre of water, weighing 1 billion metric tons, seventeen miles in the air. Would it be possible to liberate the atomic energy of a large lump of uranium more or less instantaneously, perhaps by a chain reaction in which neutrons thrown off by one nuclear fission cause fission in adjacent atoms? A number of scientists thought that it would.

So it was that in 1939, as the territorial ambitions of Nazi Germany plunged Europe deeper into the crisis that was to lead to World War II, scientists across the world stumbled across the possibility of constructing a new category of weapon of awesome destructive power. What should they do? Their solution has haunted the world ever since.

There are, in essence, three moral standpoints that it is possible to take in relation to acts of war. The first might be characterized as absolute belligerence: a belief that any act is justified in the furtherance of one's own cause and that one's own cause is unquestionably right. The second can be called absolute pacifism: its proponents will claim that no provocation can justify the use of violence as a matter of policy, even when used as a form of resistance. Adherents of these two positions are rare: Adolf Hitler and some of his more extreme followers spring to mind in the first instance; Jesus Christ and, perhaps, Mahatma Gandhi in the second. Far more common, though, is 'contingent pacifism', the belief that it is wrong to use force except in order to resist it and that the force used should be at an appropriate level; most people accept the fairness and validity of this concept and it has been almost universally enshrined as law governing the state application of violence. Thus the New York cop and the British soldier patrolling the streets of Belfast are both enjoined to use the minimum force necessary to achieve their objectives. If a British soldier in Northern Ireland saw a protestor preparing to throw a stone, he would not be entitled to shoot him or her – it would be possible, and appropriate, to attempt to arrest the protestor without significantly risking his own life; if the protestor was preparing to throw a hand grenade, however, the situation would be different: the protestor's intended action would put at risk the life of both his or her target and everybody else in the area, and the soldier would be entitled to use any force at his disposal to stop him or her, or so the law allows.

War is, of course, more complicated. Very few conflicts start with one side saying: 'We want X and we are going to use force to achieve it!' Far more often it is the continuation of an ancient quarrel, or the result of a breakdown of negotiations towards some end that is difficult to achieve. In these cases fault can be almost impossible to decide, or even irrelevant. At the same time, deciding an appropriate level of force or violence is equally problematic. Is it appropriate to attempt to kill the enemy's political leaders? Is it appropriate to kill enemy civilians? The simple answer is that one should use sufficient force to defeat aggression but, of course, in practice this represents an ethical minefield.

But as it happens World War II was not quite like that. Both Germany and Japan deliberately entered into aggression with the intention of obtaining territory and resources that they had not previously owned and in the face of both warnings and offers of negotiation. For the nations faced with their aggression, it became a fight for survival. At this decisive moment, the governments of all the major belligerent powers were approached by scientists telling them that the results of some experiments conducted in an academic laboratory in a Berlin suburb, interpreted by two refugees walking together in a snowy forest in Sweden, promised to yield weapons of extraordinary destructive power. Although the worst excesses of Nazism – particularly the systematic genocide of the Jewish population of Europe – had yet to be committed when the war was in its early days, nevertheless the grotesque reality of the regime was all too evident – especially to the many refugee scientists, of largely Jewish origin, who had managed to find sanctuary in the west. It was not surprising, therefore, that the scientific communities of Britain and the US should make a particularly compelling case to their governments about the possibilities for the new weapons and it is inconceivable that those governments would ignore such a potentially decisive advance. This explains why Britain, France, Germany, Japan and the United States all embarked on nuclear research programmes of one sort or another in the early days of the war in Europe.

Broadly speaking, the attitude of the scientists who began to research the possibilities of nuclear weapons in 1939 and 1940 was that of contingent pacifism: they were uneasy about building bombs of enormous power but they were also very concerned that their opponents – particularly the dim-witted and murderous opportunists who held sway in Germany – might get them first. The original justification that persuaded so many scientists to sign up for atomic weapons research was summed up by the Polish scientist Joseph Rotblat, who worked with Frisch at Liverpool University before going with him to Los Alamos:

> I convinced myself that the only way to stop the Germans
> from using it against us would be if we too had the bomb
> and threatened to retaliate.

It was easy to think along the same lines as Rotblat; the
calculations that had led him to conclude that a bomb
was possible were, presumably, capable of being made
just as easily in Nazi Germany as they were in Liverpool
or Berkeley. But this was not in fact the case. Although
a number of physicists of enormous international stature
remained in Germany, they reached the conclusion that a
bomb was not feasible – at least while so much industrial
effort was being taken up by the war. Which leads into
a second interesting point thrown up by the story of the
atomic bomb: the stupidity of racial prejudice.

Amongst the key personalities in the story of the atomic
bomb, the number who were refugees from the anti-
Semitism of the Third Reich and its central and southern
European allies is quite striking: Lise Meitner, Otto Frisch,
Albert Einstein, Leo Szilard, Eugene Wigner, Edward Teller,
Rudolf Peierls, Hans Bethe, Enrico Fermi and Franz Simon,
to name only a few of the most prominent, represent
an extraordinary list of concentrated scientific talent. By
concluding, on the basis of some deep-seated psychological
trauma, that Jews are in some sense more 'alien' than
any other ethnic group, Adolf Hitler effectively presented
his enemies with the most powerful weapons yet used
in warfare while eliminating any prospect that he had
of acquiring them. Nuclear scientists talk of calculating
'cross-sections' of fissile material: that is, the quantity
needed to ensure that a neutron released in one nuclear
fission will strike another nucleus and thus perpetuate the
chain reaction. By analogy, science has its own cross-section:
a scientist comes up with a hypothesis or a set of results

that he or she can take so far before it is 'released' into the wider scientific community, where other scientists have the opportunity to examine, discard or continue the work in a kind of expanding circle of creativity. Thus an idea can be like a neutron in a piece of uranium: as it travels amongst scientists, it may well be 'captured' and used to give birth to further ideas and deductions. For example, Ernest Rutherford predicted the existence of the neutron, James Chadwick found it, Hahn discovered what it did to uranium nuclei and the Los Alamos team harnessed it into an explosive.

But by forcing many of the best German scientists to leave the country because they were Jewish, and by persecuting, imprisoning and killing the rest, Hitler ensured that the 'cross-section' of German physics was reduced below the level where an idea in nuclear physics would necessarily be followed up, or a set of results accurately checked. Any hope that Nazi Germany might have had of constructing a bomb foundered on miscalculations and blunders which remained unnoticed; the principal German nuclear scientists were quietly rounded up at the end of the war and held, under surveillance, in England; confident that their research was at least the equal of that achieved by the Allies, they were amazed and dismayed to find that they were at least three years behind.

So the reason for trying to build the bomb, the fear that the enemy – Nazi Germany – might otherwise build it first, turned out to be groundless, a fact that was evident towards the end of 1944 certainly, and was a probability before then. Why then did the project continue and why was the bomb used against Japan, whose nuclear programme was way behind that even of Germany? Two principal reasons offer themselves, one cynical and financial, the other a reflection of the psychology of total war.

The Manhattan Project was stated to have cost the United States some $2,000,000,000, which was, at that time, about £500,000,000. It is a large amount of money even by today's standards, but in the 1940s it represented a colossal investment. However, for reasons of security, none of this expenditure was offered to Congress for approval; instead, the sums were hidden away amongst myriad other items in the defence budget. For Henry Stimson, Vannevar Bush, Leslie Groves and the other leading executives of the bomb project, there was a very real risk that they could find themselves facing trial for the misappropriation of federal funds if the research were abandoned or failed. The principle expenditure was on the uranium isotope separation plants at Oak Ridge and on the plutonium production reactors at Hanford, which, by late 1944, had already been built, giving the project a momentum that could not be easily overcome with the evaporation of the threat of atomic bombing from Nazi Germany. Others did feel that they could abandon work with a clear conscience; Joseph Rotblat, for example, decided that:

> when it became evident, towards the end of 1944, that the Germans had abandoned the bomb project, my work ceased to have purpose and I asked for permission to return to Britain.

But he was evidently part of a small minority and did not have a stake of $2 billion in the task. One bald truth of the atomic bomb project is that its sponsors needed to have some concrete result of their labours to show Congress or they were destined for a great deal of trouble. In the last year of the war, there is evidence of some anxiety amongst the upper echelons of the Manhattan Project that they would not have operational atomic bombs ready *before* the surrender of Japan. This is strong evidence that the atomic bomb was not thought of as in any way crucial to the ending of the war, even if it did, in the final analysis, hasten ultimate victory.

Although the formal justification for the use of the atomic bombs has always been that they removed the need for an invasion of the Japanese home islands, which had the potential to be an appalling bloodbath, there is some element of doubt that this would have been the case. Winston Churchill postulated the figure of 500,000 casualties for 'Operation Olympic', as the invasion would have been known, but other estimates were considerably lower: General MacArthur, for example, believed that he would be able to capture the southernmost island, Kyushu, with only 31,000 casualties. The atomic bombs were each expected to kill approximately 100,000 people, but these figures were projections based on incomplete knowledge. In any case, an incendiary-bomb raid on Tokyo had killed over 100,000 people in March 1945, which clearly demonstrates that the US air force in the Pacific was perfectly capable of inflicting enormous destruction without the aid of atomic weapons.*

The fact is that by the end of what had been, for the British at least, six years of war, many people were so inured to the violence and brutality that the deaths of 100,000 people could seem like a 'merciful deliverance'. Civilian populations have always suffered in war but they have rarely been made the specific targets of military

---

* The raid on Tokyo caused many more casualties than either the Hiroshima bomb, which actually had an immediate death toll of about 80,000, or the Nagasaki bomb, which killed about 45,000. This does not, of course, account for people who have since died as a result of radiation sickness and other pernicious effects of the bombs which were not obvious at the time.

action as they routinely were by the end of World War II. There is no doubt that the atomic bombings of Hiroshima and Nagasaki, together with the fire raids on Tokyo, on Dresden, on Hamburg, and the blitz on London and other British towns, were acts of enormous brutality, but within the context of the times there were clear precedents and apparent advantages to be had from carrying them out: they were, however horrendous, acts of war. To suggest, as has become fashionable recently, that they were a crime in the same sense as the Nazi genocide of Europe's Jews is to miss the point completely.

This book has been compiled for publication to coincide with the 50th anniversary of the bombing of Hiroshima, which falls on 6 August 1995. It is not by any means an attempt to produce a comprehensive history of the atomic bomb, which has been done far better elsewhere; and it should not be read as either condemnation or praise of those who decided to build and use the bomb. Instead it should be seen as a series of snapshots of what the people who were actually involved in the whole story saw at the time and reported later. Where there is a dearth of direct eye-witness material I have filled the gaps with my own narrative, drawn from various excellent histories of the many aspects of the story.

It is to be hoped that there is no repeat of the atomic bombings of Hiroshima and Nagasaki. In times of comparative peace, even the simple possession of the weapons capable of inflicting such damage can seem appalling, but the truth is that there is no going back now. The American officer who flew the first atomic bomb to Hiroshima said later that he felt that the scientists of Los Alamos had given him a look inside Pandora's box; he was quite right, but, like Pandora's box, the contents once released could not be returned. Nuclear weapons are with us now and have often, in the past fifty years, seemed an appalling menace; but there was undoubtedly a time when they appeared to answer the prayers of the beleaguered nations of the free world.

List of Illustrations

1

Scientific Background

On 4 August 1945, Colonel Paul Tibbets was briefing a group of United States aircrew on the small Pacific island of Tinian:

The colonel began by saying that whatever any of us, including himself, had done before was small potatoes compared to what we were going to do now. Then he said the usual things, but he said them well, as if he meant them, about how proud he was to have been associated with us, about how high our morale had been, and how difficult it was not knowing what we were doing, thinking maybe we were wasting our time and that the 'gimmick' was just somebody's wild dream. He was personally honoured and he was sure all of us were, to have been chosen to take part in this raid, which, he said – and all the other big-wigs nodded when he said it – would shorten the war by at least six months.

(Sergeant Abe Spitzer, radio operator,
509th Composite Bomber Group)

Two days later, in the early hours of 6 August, the same

colonel was talking to a different sergeant in the waist compartment of a B-29 bomber en route to Japan:

> I remembered something else, and just as the last of the old man was disappearing, I sort of tugged at his foot, which was still showing. He came sliding back in a hurry, thinking maybe something was wrong. 'What's the matter?'
>
> I looked at him and said, 'Colonel, are we splitting atoms today?'
>
> This time he gave me a really funny look, and said, 'That's about it.'
>
> (Sergeant Robert Caron, tail gunner, Enola Gay)

A few hours later, just after a quarter past eight, Tibbets remembered:

> A bright light filled the plane. The first shock wave hit us.

His co-pilot, Robert Lewis, wrote in his diary:

> If I live a hundred years, I'll never quite get these few moments out of my mind.

In the city below, the writer Yoko Ota:

> could not understand why our surroundings had changed so greatly in one instant . . . I thought it might have been something which had nothing to do with the war, the collapse of the earth which it was said would take place at the end of the world.

It had taken a long time for human understanding of the

fundamental nature of matter to get from the first faint insights of 'natural philosophers' to the chain reaction over Hiroshima. The idea that matter might consist of a myriad of tiny, indivisible particles was first aired in the fifth century BC in classical Greece. Leucippus of Miletus, a town on the coast of Asia Minor (in modern-day Turkey), and his intellectual follower Democritus of Abdera (in Thrace), hypothesized that such varying properties as colour, hardness, mass and heat were the result of different arrangements of these particles, or *atoma*. Democritus had no place in his intellectual scheme for supernatural influences, mythical gods or any form of 'guiding intelligence'; for him, there was simply the blind interplay of flying and colliding atoms:

> Apparently there is colour, apparently sweetness, apparently bitterness; actually there are only atoms and the void.
>
> (Democritus, *c*.420 BC)

Although virtually none of the writings of the original 'atomist' philosophers have survived in their original form, Epicurus of Samos (341–270 BC), who taught in Athens, wrote extensively on the atomist theory, and this work was transmitted to the Roman world by the poet Lucretius in his long poem *De rerum natura* ('On the nature of things'), written originally in the first century BC, and rediscovered and published in 1473.

Epicurus grafted several new features onto atomism. One (much criticized by his contemporaries) was the theory of 'swerve', which allowed atoms to deviate slightly from their expected 'track', thus preserving free will for humanity (after all, if everything in the universe is the result of the collisions and alignments of atoms with a predictable range of movements, claiming that human thought and decision making is a result of free will is nonsensical). Another allowed the 'hooks' of one atom sometimes to catch the 'eyes' of another, thus providing the mechanism for the formation of larger bodies.

Atomic theory made little progress beyond Epicurus for many centuries and it was, in any case, far from being accepted as fact – notable opponents included, for example, Aristotle – but it did provide a reasonable theoretical basis for the kind of everyday observations that the natural philosophers of the pre-scientific era would make: the dissolving of salts in water; the gradual diffusion of coloured dyes into solutions; the evaporation of liquids; and the formation and disappearance of mists and clouds. Those who came to support it included Isidore of Seville (c.AD 560–636), the English monk Bede (c.AD 673–735), the French philosopher Pierre Gassendi (1592–1655), John Locke (in his *Essay Concerning Human Understanding*, 1690) and Robert Hooke, who suggested in 1678 that the 'elasticity' of a gas was the result of collisions of its atoms with the walls of its container. It was also adopted by Sir Isaac Newton (1642–1727), who was much interested in the theories and speculations of the ancients. In 1718 he wrote:

> It seems probable to me that God in the beginning formed matter in solid, massy, hard, impenetrable, movable particles, of such sizes and figures, and with such other properties, and in such proportion, as most conduced to the end for which he formed them.

But in reality, despite the occasional near-misses scored by the early natural philosophers, atomic theories did not make a great contribution to the advancement of human knowledge until the arrival of rational, empirical, experiment-based science towards the end of the eighteenth century. Science until then was simply the application of strict logic to the observable phenomena of the everyday world – like apples falling from trees. Before the acceptance of 'the scientific method' (the formal process by which a theory is tested by controlled experiment and thus proved or disproved), alchemists, metallurgists, pharmacists and a host of even less plausible charlatans, con men and lunatics made do with a ramshackle collection of bizarre doctrines: seven particular metals were associated with the seven known planets; base metals could be transmuted into gold; the four elements were declared to be water, air, fire and earth; and, as an example of 'applied science', underground mines were occasionally sealed to allow time for the further growth of metals.

The great revolution in the empirical, physical sciences that eventually led to the 'light of a thousand suns' shining over Hiroshima began in the eighteenth century, and it took place in chemistry; but an important forerunner was Robert Boyle (1627–91), whose precise measurement of how the volume of a gas is affected by a change of pressure and temperature is still described in school textbooks ('Boyle's law', etc.). In his book *The Sceptical Chymist*, he gave an early definition of *elements* (nowadays defined as: 'any of the substances that cannot be resolved by chemical means into simpler substances') that successfully distinguished them from the chemical *compounds* which are composed of two or more elements in combination. Building on Boyle's work, the great French chemist Lavoisier (1745–94), who met his end on the guillotine during the Revolution, emphasized the new willingness to experiment empirically in his definition of elements:

we must admit as elements all the substances into which

we are capable, by any means, to reduce bodies during decomposition. Not that we can be certain that these substances we consider as simple may not be compounded of two, or even a greater number of principles; but, since these principles cannot be separated, or rather since we have not hitherto discovered the means of separating them, they act with regard to us as simple substances, and we ought never to suppose them compounded until experiment and observation have proved them to be so . . .

(Traité élémentaire de chimie, 1789)

Essentially, Lavoisier's statement outlines an approach that is both workable and consistent and, if rigorously applied, would deal with the problem more than adequately. But in the table of elements or 'simple substances' that was published with it, Lavoisier unconsciously illustrated the need for critical rigour by including, together with the true elements, a number of compound substances and such items as 'light' and 'caloric'.

With genuine logical self-awareness, Lavoisier also remarked:

if by the term 'elements' we mean to express those simple and indivisible atoms of which matter is composed, it seems extremely probable that we know nothing at all about them.

Lavoisier's insight was, at that time, undeniably true, but this ignorance was soon to yield under the impetus of a number of discoveries as the new experiment-based chemistry took hold. In Scotland, Joseph Black (1728–99) showed that limestone and other mild alkalis released 'fixed air' (or carbon dioxide) when decomposed by acids, whilst Joseph

Priestley of Birmingham published, in 1774, his discovery of a 'new' gas, oxygen, which he found to be a component of ordinary air and essential to life. Priestley's work enabled Lavoisier to clear up the confusion surrounding the nature of fire and combustion, demonstrating that these were simple chemical reactions in which oxygen combines with other elements, generating heat and light.

In 1789, as the search for new elements continued, a German chemist, Martin Klaproth, who was later to become the first professor of chemistry in Berlin, discovered a new metal of very high density. He decided to name it uranium after the planet Uranus, discovered by William Herschel in 1781.

As new substances were added to the table of elements, others were removed. Humphry Davy showed 'soda' and 'potash' to be compounds of the two highly reactive new metals sodium and potassium, and Henry Cavendish showed water to be a compound of hydrogen and oxygen.

As the rate at which chemists unlocked the secrets of the composition of chemical compounds increased, it became increasingly apparent that they needed an overall framework within which to place the elements that they had discovered. This was ultimately provided by John Dalton (1766–1844), the son of a Quaker hand-loom weaver. Using the discovery that elements in chemical compounds were always in simple numerical ratios to one another in a 'law of constant proportion', he announced a 'law of multiple proportion', which stated, in basic terms, that different chemical compounds can be made from the same two elements if the elements are in different proportion to each other (a good example of this is carbon monoxide and carbon dioxide, both simple compounds of carbon and oxygen). Dalton's great achievement was to realize that the growing body of well-attested experimental facts could be systematized through a revival of the ancient atomic theory. He saw that it should be possible to establish the weight of each different kind of atom, relative to the weight of some chosen standard element, such as hydrogen. These values would be a guide in research on the composition of chemical substances, and on new chemical reactions.

The basic principles of Dalton's theory were that each chemical element is made up of a quantity of indivisible atoms of the same fixed mass; that the atoms of different elements have different masses; and that the ultimate particles of a compound (called 'molecules') are also identical and are made up of a small, fixed number of atoms of more than one element.

As the nineteenth century progressed, it was found that a certain amount of elaboration was required for some of Dalton's rules in particular cases, but even so, the German scientist Justus von Liebig was able to write in 1854:

> All our ideas are so dependent on the Daltonian theory that we cannot imagine ourselves back in a time when it did not exist . . . the atomic theory gave Chemistry a fundamental view which overruled and governed all other theoretical views . . . its extraordinary service was to supply a fertile soil for further progress, which was previously lacking.

By 1869, about 64 chemical elements were recognized and their atomic weights were found to range from hydrogen (= 1) to uranium (= 238) in ascending order. An observation that was made by several scientists was that elements with certain similar properties recurred at regular intervals in the series. This idea was pre-eminently developed by the Russian scientist Dmitri Mendeleyev of St Petersburg.

Mendeleyev was born in 1834 in Tobolsk, Siberia, the youngest of fourteen children. In 1848, he and his mother walked to Moscow together so that he could continue his education, only to find that he was required to go instead to St Petersburg; they walked there as well! Although highly educated and a scientist of genius, he retained many Siberian customs, including having his hair and beard cut just once a year.

Mendeleyev's principal achievement was the construction of a rectangular table displaying the elements in ten horizontal rows in order of increasing atomic weight. Although hydrogen occupied a unique position on its own, the eight columns (or 'groups') in Mendeleyev's table could be seen to be occupied by elements of similar characteristics. In order for this to work, it was necessary for Mendeleyev to leave a few spaces blank; nevertheless he was able to predict a number of properties that the elements that should occupy the blank spaces would have. The discovery of gallium, scandium and germanium between 1875 and 1886 filled some of the gaps in Mendeleyev's table, and the close agreement of their properties with those that had been predicted caused a sensation amongst scientists. Mendeleyev himself told the Chemical Society in London in 1889:

> Before the promulgation of the periodic law the chemical elements were mere fragmentary, incidental facts in nature; there was no special reason to expect the discovery of new elements and the new ones that were discovered from time to time appeared to be possessed of quite novel properties.

Mendeleyev's Table was soon widely adopted. It has been through successive revisions and enlargements (still retaining the quaint adjective 'Periodic' in its title) and remains the symbol and enduring pictograph of chemical science. It was not seriously questioned even when it was discovered that a sequence of fourteen metallic elements, with atomic weights from 140 to 175, and having similar chemical properties, began at lanthanum and ended at lutetium. This block of so-called 'rare earth' elements is an obvious breakdown of 'periodicity', but was treated as anomaly, for which an explanation would one day be found – as indeed it was, with the electron-shell theory of atomic structure in 1913.

The marshalling of the elements in order of atomic mass, and in this rectangular array of the Table shows a tendency to order and repetition in chemical properties which is strongly suggestive of some underlying, more fundamental, structure. One such property is the typical valence of each element; the power of its atoms to combine with one, two, three, four or more other atoms. The means by which this joining together of atoms is achieved was then not known, but some evidence about the chemical bonds formed by carbon atoms had been obtained.

Many kinds of carbon-containing molecules were found in plant and animal cells, the carbon atoms being chiefly combined with atoms of hydrogen, oxygen and nitrogen, but also with others. To account for the existence of this variety, two young chemists, F. A. Kekulé of Germany and A. S. Couper, a Scot working in Paris, deduced independently (1858) that carbon atoms normally have four valencies, and are able to bond together into long chains and branched chains of atoms and also into closed rings. In 1874, J. H. Van't Hoff of Holland and J. A. Le Bel of France also demonstrated, from the chemical evidence, that the four valencies of a carbon atom do not lie in the same geometric plane but are directed symmetrically outwards from the centre, in three dimensions, as if towards the vertices of a tetrahedron.

These findings pointed the way to the accurate spatial representation of the structures of millions of different molecules, eventually including such complex examples as carbohydrates, proteins and DNA. This new science brought novel processes into such industries as dyestuffs, pharmaceuticals and explosives. The Swedish chemist and engineer Alfred Nobel (1833–96) made a fortune from the invention of dynamite (1866) and of blasting gelatine (1875). An unexpected 'spin-off' was his establishment of the prestigious Nobel prizes, given annually for physics and chemistry, for physiology and medicine, for literature and for peace (and first awarded in 1901).

By the mid-nineteenth century the atomic theory, with its emphasis on the relative masses of different atoms, had led to much progress in chemistry. Most chemists were inclined to believe that atoms, although invisible and intangible, really existed. There were some exceptions such as H. E. Roscoe, professor at Manchester from 1857, who remarked: 'Atoms are round bits of wood invented by Mr Dalton.'

Physics had not, in the early decades of the century, been much influenced by these developments. The earlier triumphs of Galileo and Newton had been followed by the work of Huygens and Young on the wave theory of light. Joseph Black, a Scot born in Bordeaux, had begun scientific studies of the nature of heat by devising accurate ways of measuring 'quantity of heat' and 'specific heat'. A generation later, Michael Faraday (1791–1867) embarked on his famous series of 'Experimental Researches on Electricity and Magnetism', published over a forty-year span.

The path which led physicists to embrace atomic theory started from the work of Black. Improvements in the design of steam engines as a source of motive power (for example, by James Watt, 1736–1819) gave rise to the exact studies of James Joule (1818–89) on the relationship between heat and mechanical work. On this basis the French physicist Sadi Carnot (1796–1832) and William Thomson, later Lord

Kelvin (1824–1907), established the fundamental science of classical thermodynamics.

Thermodynamics is independent of hypotheses about the nature of matter, but the successes of atomic theory in chemistry revived interest in an old view that the temperature of a sample is simply a measure of the energy of motion of its atoms or molecules. The existence of a perpetual 'commotion among the invisible small parts of bodies' could account for the pressure of a gas in a container, and explain why it increases when the temperature is raised.

First attempts to calculate the properties of gases by applying Newton's mechanics to a system containing a large number of moving and colliding particles were only partially successful. It had not been realized that the molecules do not all have roughly the same velocity. The incessant mutual collisions in fact produce a very wide range of velocities. The difficulty was resolved by James Clerk Maxwell (1831–79) in 1859, when he was professor at King's College, London, by an application of the mathematical theory of probability. His calculations of the motions of molecules in air at 60°F (15.5°C) revealed an astonishing submicroscopic universe of very small, fast-moving particles.

He found the average speed of the molecules is 1,505 feet (459 metres) per second; that each molecule makes an average 8,077,200,000 collisions per second; and that their 'mean free path' (the average distance that they travel between one collision and the next) is 56.8 nanometers (56.8 metres divided by 1,000,000,000). Maxwell also calculated that if the pressure (and density) of air were increased or decreased many-fold, its viscosity would remain unchanged. This prediction, which was contrary to general supposition, was soon verified by experiment.

The diameters of individual gas molecules (which in some cases are single atoms) may be calculated from this kinetic theory. The values obtained for gaseous elements such as nitrogen, oxygen, hydrogen and argon are close to 0.3 nanometers.

These minute dimensions stand in contrast with the very large value of Avogadro's Number, which is also derived from the kinetic theory. This quantity is the number of atoms or molecules contained in the mass of an element or compound which is equal to the atomic or molecular weight expressed in grams; for example, 12 grams of carbon, or 44 grams of carbon dioxide.

The Number is $6.022\ 05 \times 10^{23}$ atoms (or molecules) in 1 gram mole; or (approximately) 6 followed by 23 noughts. It is too large to be easily comprehended. As an illustration, Sir James Jeans (1877–1946), the physicist and writer on science, estimated that if all the molecules in a glass of water were turned into grains of sand there would be sufficient to cover the entire United States of America to a depth of about 30 metres.

Maxwell, who ranks as the most able theoretical physicist of the nineteenth century, retired from King's College in 1865 (aged 34) to his small family estate in Scotland. Here he wrote his famous *Treatise on Electricity and Magnetism*, which included the electromagnetic theory of light and the prediction of radio waves. He emerged in 1871 to be the first Cavendish professor at Cambridge, where he directed the new laboratory until his death in 1879. His work on statistical mechanics was extended by Ludwig Boltzmann of Vienna (1844–1906), who ensured the final acceptance, in physics, of the atomic hypothesis. Boltzmann's equation, $S = k \log W$, which relates the thermodynamic entropy S to the statistical probability W, was carved on his tomb.

Another unexplained property of atoms which was investigated in detail in the mid-nineteenth century was the emission of radiation in the visible spectrum when strongly heated. It was long known that different metallic salts impart different colours to a flame. In 1822 John Herschel used Newton's technique of spreading out the spectrum by means of a glass prism. He found spectra consisting of a number of narrow, bright lines separated by dark spaces (in contrast to the continuous 'rainbow' spectrum obtained by Newton from sunlight).

At Heidelberg, R. W. Bunsen and G. R. Kirchhoff measured the positions and wave lengths of the lines with a spectroscope, and found them to be uniquely characteristic for each element. From 1859 onwards, spectroscopic analysis was employed as a sensitive and powerful new tool. In 1868 the astronomers Janssen and Lockyer examined the spectrum of the sun's photosphere during an eclipse, and observed a yellow line which did not belong to any known substance. Lockyer concluded that it must belong to a new element, to which he gave the name helium (Greek *helios*, 'the sun').

About twenty-five years later, Lord Rayleigh, at Cambridge, observed that 'pure' nitrogen obtained from the atmosphere was significantly more dense than nitrogen obtained from chemical compounds. In collaboration with William Ramsay at University College, London, it was found (1894) that when nitrogen from the air was reacted chemically with red-hot magnesium, or by sparking with oxygen, a small residue of another gas remained. It did not react chemically with any other elements, and its specific heat showed its molecules to be monatomic. It was given the name argon (Greek, 'inert'). Its atomic weight is 39.9, close to potassium. Ramsay speculated that argon compounds might be found in minerals. He obtained a gram of the Norwegian uranium-bearing mineral cleveite, which contains a gas then thought to be nitrogen. Treating the solid with sulphuric acid, he obtained gas, but its spectrum was neither that of nitrogen nor that of argon.

He provisionally labelled it krypton ('hidden') and sent it for analysis to Sir William Crookes (March 1985). He received by telegram the reply 'Krypton is helium.' The gas was the unknown element first discovered in the sun by Janssen and Lockyer; it was chemically unreactive, and monatomic; and its atomic weight was 4, placing it before lithium in the table of elements.

Ramsay inferred that there must be a complete group of inert gases. A two-year investigation of minerals disclosed no new elements, but liquid air then became available and could be separated into light and heavy fractions. In May, June and July 1898, three new gases were isolated from it: krypton, atomic weight 83.8; neon ('the new one'), atomic weight 20.2 (which emitted 'a blaze of crimson light' when examined spectroscopically); and xenon ('stranger') with atomic weight 131.3.

Both helium and xenon feature in the development of nuclear physics, as does the heaviest inert gas, radon (atomic weight 222), which was identified by Rutherford in 1900 and shown by Soddy to belong to the argon group.

The discovery of the inert gases was a brilliant episode in the history of physics and chemistry. There were clearly questions still to be answered in many fields (among them, how atoms contrived to emit light of such sharply defined wavelengths). But as the century ended some physicists voiced the thought that perhaps not very much really new science still awaited research.

Within twelve years they were contradicted by events. A burst of far-reaching experimental and theoretical developments transformed 'nineteenth-century physics' into 'modern physics', and set the world on course towards atomic fission.

Attempts in the eighteenth century to find out the nature of electricity included the famous experiments of Benjamin

Frankin (1706–90) of Philadelphia. In the nineteenth century, both Faraday and Maxwell came close to considering the electric current to be a stream of charged corpuscles but did not commit themselves. Others took the view that it was some type of wave motion which, like light and radiant heat, could cross empty space.

Experiments centred on electrical conduction in gases at low pressures. It was thought that the true nature of the current might be more easily discerned if complications due to the gas molecules were minimized. The usual arrangement (a primitive ancestor of TV tubes and visual display units) consisted of a closed glass tube having two wires sealed through its wall to connect to a negatively charged cathode and a positive anode. Most of the air could be removed from the tube through a connection to a vacuum pump.

In 1858–9 Julius Plusker of Bonn, using an efficient new pump designed by Johann Geissler, saw that at low pressure no light remained in the tube except for a greenish glow near the cathode, which he thought might be the electric current itself. A succession of investigators followed in his footsteps. Goldstein found that the nature of the residual gas and the electrode metals had no effect on the greenish glow, which also appeared on the glass near the anode. The glow, which he named 'cathode rays' (1876), did appear to cross the near-vacuum and energize the glass opposite.

Crookes, and also Hittorf, confirmed that the rays cast shadows of objects in their path. H. R. Hertz (1857–94) of Hamburg and Bonn (who discovered radio waves a few years later) found, in 1883, that when rays passed between oppositely charged metal plates they were not deflected. This indicated that they were a wave motion, like light, and not charged particles; but Perrin (1895) found that they did deposit a negative charge on contact with a surface.

J. J. Thomson (1856–1940), a Fellow of Trinity College,

had been elected to the Cavendish Professorship in 1884. He believed that the cathode rays were negatively charged particles, and that Hertz's failure to deflect them was due to their high velocity. In 1897, using improved pumps and higher voltages on the plates, he found a deflection of the rays towards the positive plate. He showed that a magnet also deflects the rays, which are therefore streams of particles, and he was able to measure the degree of deflection in both cases.

From his results, by an ingenious calculation, Thomson obtained the ratio of the charge on the new particle to its mass. He then derived the mass, on the assumption (soon confirmed) that the charge has the same value as that carried by ordinary anions, such as the chloride ion.

He had named the new negative particle the electron, and now had the remarkable result that the mass of an electron is only a small fraction (about 1/1830) of that of the hydrogen atom. It was the first subatomic particle to be identified:

> At first there were very few who believed in the existence of these bodies smaller than atoms. I was even told long afterwards by a distinguished physicist who had been present [in 1897] at my lecture at the Royal Institution that he thought I had been 'pulling their legs'.
>
> (J. J. Thomson, *Recollections and Reflections*, 1936)

Thomson was awarded the Nobel prize for physics in 1906, and is buried near Newton in Westminster Abbey. His son, G. P. Thomson (1892–1975), shared a Nobel prize in 1937 for showing, as he somewhat ironically remarked, that the electron is not only a particle, but also a wave.

In 1895 at Wurzburg, W. K. Roentgen (1845–1923) was studying the luminescence caused by cathode rays when they impinged on sheets of paper coated with a suitable chemical. He made the chance observation that sheets of the paper elsewhere in the laboratory also glowed when the apparatus was switched on. When he took some paper into the next room it again glowed, in spite of the intervening wall.

Whatever was producing the effect travelled in straight lines, cast shadows and was much more penetrating than the cathode rays, (passing easily through some materials, but stopped by others). It also blackened photographic plates. Roentgen called it 'X-rays', which was an apt a name as any, and he showed more publicity consciousness than many contemporary scientists. In the two months before Christmas 1895 he took 'shadow' photographs of the interiors of many objects and wrote an article for the Wurzburg scientific society, which was printed as a ten-page pamphlet. Copies were sent to all the leading European physicists, together with photographs of the skeletal structure inside living bodies.

The first X-ray pictures were published in the Vienna newspapers and caused a great sensation. Roentgen received one of the first Nobel prizes in 1901, largely because of the immense potential of his discovery for the field of medicine. Its importance for other branches of science was at least as great, but was realized more slowly. In 1912 the German physicist Max von Laue (1879–1960) showed that X-rays were electromagnetic radiation of the same nature as visible light, but that they have very much shorter wavelengths. In 1913 W. H. Bragg (1862–1942) and his son W. L. Bragg (1890–1971) at the Cavendish laboratory measured X-ray wavelengths in the range between 1/50 and 1/50,000 of the wavelengths of visible light. The Braggs used X-rays with great success in deducing the spatial arrangement of atoms in the crystals of many different chemical compounds. The X-ray study of crystalline DNA by Rosalind Franklin (1920–58) at Kings College, London, was a vital contribution to knowledge of genes, and the beginning of modern molecular biology, in 1953.

One of the earliest studies of the physical effects of X-rays was initiated by J. J. Thomson towards the end of 1895, when the first research students were coming into the Cavendish:

> I had a copy of [Roentgen's] apparatus made . . . and the first thing I did with it was to see what effect the passage of these rays through a gas would produce on its electrical properties. To my great delight I found that this made it a conductor of electricity, even though the electric force applied to the gas was exceedingly small, whereas the gas when it was not exposed to the rays did not conduct electricity unless the electric force were increased many thousandfold . . . The X-rays seemed to turn the gas into a gaseous electrolyte . . . There is an interval when the gas conducts though the rays had ceased to go through it. We studied the properties of the gas in this state, and found that the conductivity was destroyed when the gas passed through a filter of glass wool.
>
> A still more interesting discovery was that the conductivity could be filtered out without using any mechanical filter, by exposing the conducting gas to electric forces. The first experiments show that the conductivity is due to the particles present in the gas, and the second shows that these particles are charged with electricity. The conductivity die to the Roentgen rays is caused by these rays producing in the gas a number of charged particles.

(J. J. Thomson, *Recollections and Reflections*, 1936)

This preliminary study gave a good indication that the effect of X-rays on molecules is to eject electrons or to rupture chemical bonds, in either case producing pairs of oppositely charged ions, which allow the gas to conduct electricity. Exposure of tissue to ionizing radiation (and to ionizing particles) can cause biological damage, sometimes irreversible, and some early researchers with X-rays became seriously ill through over-exposure. A varying level of 'background' radiation is found everywhere, and is supplemented by cosmic radiation from space. There is evidently a level which human bodies can tolerate, but which depends on a complex of factors not yet fully defined.

Fundamental advances in physics were made in quick succession near the end of the nineteenth-century. The discovery of radioactivity was the breakthrough which led on, in turn, to the concepts of the nuclear atom, nuclear physics, nuclear fission and the atomic bomb. This process would have been considerably retarded but for two new theoretical developments of great originality, which were formulated by Max Planck and by Albert Einstein. These introduced totally novel perspectives into physical thought, and proved powerful tools for interpreting the unexpected new results which came from the experimentalists.

The quantum theory was the unexpected product of studies of the way in which hot bodies give out or absorb radiant heat. A piece of steel that is only warm emits heat by radiation in the infra-red part of the spectrum. As its temperature is increased it starts to radiate shorter wavelengths in the visible spectrum, and its colour changes from cherry, to orange, to yellow, to white. At its hottest it radiates in all the visible spectrum, and in the ultra-violet.

The question studied was: what is the total amount of energy being radiated away at various different (constant) temperatures? And how much of the total energy, at any particular temperature, is carried by different sections of the wavelength spectrum? In classical physics the process was pictured (very reasonably) as due to large numbers of tiny oscillators, which picked up vibrational energy in the hot solid, and then radiated it away as electromagnetic waves. The theory predicted that the amount radiated should be low at the longer wavelengths, greater at intermediate wavelengths, and much greater in the ultra-violet region.

Experiments showed that this was not so. More energy was radiated at intermediate wavelengths than in the red or the ultra-violet. Attempts to modify the theory to fit the facts did not succeed, and the discrepancy so disturbed some physicists that they called it the 'ultra-violet catastrophe'.

The remarkable solution to the problem was found in 1900 by Max Planck (1858–1947), professor of physics at Berlin:

> Planck knew how revolutionary the idea was the day he had it, because on that day he took his little boy for one of those professorial walks that academics take after lunch all over the world, and said to him, "I have had a conception today as revolutionary and as great as the kind of thought that Newton had.' And so it was.
>
> (J. Bronowski)

He realized that theory would fit experiment if there were a restriction on the amount of energy which an oscillator could radiate or absorb. The energy of a vibrating or oscillating system is proportional to its frequency (number of vibrations per second), usually denoted by v (Greek *nu*). Planck therefore wrote: Energy = hv (h times v) in which h is a universal constant of nature; and he stated that the energy of a system which has a particular frequency, v, has to be a whole-number multiple of the packet or 'quantum' hv. The system can only emit or absorb energy in amounts of hv, $2hv$, $3hv$ . . . etc.

Planck's constant, h, was found to have the value 6.626

$\times$ 10^{-34}, that is to say about 6.6 divided by the enormous number of 1 followed by 34 noughts. An individual quantum of energy is therefore exceedingly small, but its value depends on the frequency. A radio transmitter operating on a wavelength of 1,500 metres uses a frequency of 200,000 cycles per second (200 kilohertz), and each quantum (also called a 'photon' in electromagnetic radiation) has the minute energy of 1.33×10^{-28} joules.

A typical photon of blue light (frequency 7.5×10^{14} cycles per second) has energy equal to 5×10^{-19} joules. To compare this with the energies of chemical reactions (normally expressed as joules per gram molecule), it has to be multiplied by Avogadro's Number. The result is 300 kilojoules per mole, which is quite sufficient to initiate many photochemical reactions.

X-rays have considerably higher frequencies and, on the same basis, the quanta are equivalent to many thousands of kilojoules. This accords with their damaging effects on complex biological molecules, and their disruption of ordered solid structures.

Planck and other physicists were dubious at first about the 'atomization' of energy, and supposed it might only be applicable to the problem of heat radiation. However, the new concept was used by Albert Einstein in 1905 to give a detailed explanation of the 'photoelectric effect', in which light quanta eject electrons from metallic surfaces.

The quantum theory has since been used to solve many of the problems of atomic physics and of matter in bulk. Niels Bohr, a Danish physicist (1885–1962), employed it to give a very accurate quantitative account of the atomic spectrum of hydrogen, and it has proved essential to the understanding of electrical conduction metals, transistors and semiconductors.

Albert Einstein (1879–1955), born in Bavaria, of Jewish

parents, was educated at Munich and Zurich. He took Swiss nationality in 1901 and worked as an examiner in the Swiss patent office at Berne from 1902 to 1905. He was head of the Kaiser Wilhelm Institute for Physics in Berlin from 1914 to 1933, but left Germany on Hitler's rise to power, going first to Oxford, and then to Princeton University.

His special (1905) and general (1916) theories of relativity constitute a new conception of the universe, going beyond Newton's theory of the late seventeenth century (although this is quite accurate enough for the navigation of space vehicles and the positioning of artificial satellites in the solar system). It proved difficult to devise experiments to check the accuracy of Einstein's predictions, but in the case of the orbit of Mercury, the planet nearest to the sun, this was possible. The orbit is not a perfect ellipse because of the gravitational influence of the other planets, and Newtonian mechanics does not describe the real orbit accurately, but Einstein's theory is exact.

Because of the theory's importance to physics, a second check was needed, and when World War I had ended, the Royal Society of London sent expeditions to Brazil and the west coast of Africa to observe the eclipse of 29 May 1919. The theory of relativity predicted that the gravitational field near the sun would bend inwards a ray of light coming from a distant star. To an observer on earth, seeing light just passing the rim of the sun, there would be an apparent displacement of the distant object. The astronomer and astrophysicist Sir Arthur Eddington was in charge of the African expedition, and always considered his first measurement of the photographs taken there to be the greatest moment of his life. One of the messages received in London read:

Einstein's theory is completely confirmed. The predicted

displacement was 1".72 and the observed 1".75±0.06 [*the numbers are in seconds of arc*].

One of the new predictions which could not then (1905) be verified is summarized by the relationship: $E = mc^2$. In this, E stands for energy, m for mass and c^2 for the square of the velocity of light (a very large number). It implies that if a relatively small amount of mass is destroyed by conversion into energy, a very large amount of energy will be created. Within one generation it was shown that this relationship explains the ability of stars to generate and radiate enormous amounts of energy for many millions of years. It was also realized that the conversion of matter directly into energy could perhaps be achieved on earth. No practical possibility of doing so was discerned until 1939, when it emerged as a by-product of purely academic research in nuclear physics.

The key discovery that atoms of some of the heaviest elements are naturally unstable was made by the French physicist Antoine Becquerel (1852–1908), professor at the École Polytechnique. He had worked on chemical compounds which are caused to fluoresce by light, and on learning of Roentgen's X-rays he tried to find whether they are also produced during fluorescence. The results at first were negative, but in February 1896 he used a uranium salt as the fluorescing substance. It was placed in the sunlight on the top of a photographic plate that was wrapped in heavy black paper. When the plate was developed it had become darkened, as if X-rays in the fluorescence had penetrated the paper.

Further experiments showed that this was not the case. The 'radioactivity', as Becquerel named it (March 1896), occurred without any illumination by light, and the salt used did not need to be fluorescent; the only requirement was that uranium should be one of its component atoms. In May he showed that a piece of fairly pure metallic uranium would also darken the photographic plate. The very surprising conclusion was that the steady output of unidentified radiation comes from the uranium atoms alone, and without any external stimulus. It was not altered by heat or chemical treatment.

Becquerel did not take his research further at that time, but in 1897 work on the problem was begun by Madame Curie (née Marya Sklodowska). Marie Curie (1867–1934) was born in Warsaw, in part of Poland that had been annexed by Russia. She came to Paris in 1891 and obtained degrees in physics and mathematics at the Sorbonne. She married Pierre Curie (1859–1906), a physicist, in 1895, and began doctoral research, in Paris, on radioactivity. She tested metals, minerals and manufactured chemicals, using an electrometer devised by Pierre. The only substance which was radioactive was pitchblende, the ore from which uranium is extracted, but, astonishingly, the ore gave out radiation more intense than that from pure uranium.

The Curies surmised that an unknown radioactive element must also be present, and embarked on a very laborious chemical separation process. The gradual separation and concentration of not one, but two, new radioactive elements was traced, stage by stage, by measurements of the radiation from different fractions. The first they named polonium; and the discovery of the second, radium, was announced on 26 December 1898.

The amounts involved were minute and were identified by their radiation. To obtain visible quantities, sufficient for further study, they repeated the extraction process, starting with one ton of pitchblende residues, and in 1902, after four years, obtained one tenth of a gram of almost pure radium chloride. The pure metal is about a million times more radioactive than uranium, and its atomic weight was found to be 226.4.

This heroic endeavour was carried through to success under difficult conditions and in spite of a known, but then unquantified, health hazard:

Pierre Curie always had very restricted facilities for his work and in fact one can say he never had a conventional laboratory at his complete disposition. As director of the classes at the School of Physics he could use for his research, to the extent that the needs of the instruction permitted, the resources of the teaching laboratory; he often expressed his gratitude for the liberty allowed him in this regard. But in this laboratory for pupils no room was assigned especially to him; the place that most often served as his refuge was a narrow passage between a staircase and a preparation room; it was here that he did his extensive work on magnetism. Later he obtained authorisation to use a glassed-in work shop situated on the ground floor of the school and serving as a storeroom and machine shop. It was in this shop that our researches on radioactivity began. We could not think of carrying out chemical operations there without damaging the machines: those operations were organised in an abandoned shed opposite the machine shop, which had formerly sheltered the practical work of the medical school. In this shed with an asphalt floor, whose glass roof offered us only incomplete protection against the rain, which was like a greenhouse in summer and which an iron stove barely heated in winter, we passed the best and happiest years of our existence, consecrating our entire days to the work. Deprived of all the conveniences that facilitate the work of the chemist, we carried out there with great difficulty a large number of treatments on increasing quantities of material. When the operations could not be performed outside, open windows allowed the poisonous vapours to escape. The only equipment consisted of some old tables of well worn pine on which I disposed my precious fractions from the concentration of radium. Having no cabinet to enclose the radiant products obtained, we placed them on the tables or on planks, and I remember the delight we experienced when we happened to enter our domain at night and saw on all sides the palely luminescent silhouettes of the products of our work.

(Marie Curie in the preface to the
Collected Works of Pierre Curie)

The Curies and Becquerel shared the 1903 Nobel prize in physics. Pierre Curie was killed in a traffic accident in Paris in April 1906. The 1911 Nobel prize (for the discovery of two elements) went therefore to Marie alone. She died in 1934 of leukemia, possibly the result of long exposure to radioactivity.

A new figure, Ernest Rutherford (1871–1937), now came on the scene from New Zealand. A physicist who won a scholarship to Cambridge in 1894, he worked with J. J. Thomson on the radioactivity of uranium, and the ionization produced by the rays. He showed that the rays from uranium were a mixture of two different kinds, which he labelled 'alpha' and 'beta'. The alpha rays produced much ionization in gases but had little penetration, and were stopped by a single sheet of paper. The beta rays penetrated more like X-rays, but, compared with X-rays, produced rather feeble ionization.

In 1898, with Thomson's support, Rutherford obtained an appointment as research professor at McGill University in Canada. In the same year Mme Curie, in Paris, discovered that thorium is also radioactive, and Rutherford arranged for some salts of thorium and uranium to be sent to him in Montreal.

Rutherford, with the electrical engineer R. B. Owens, studied the radioactivity of thorium oxide. The measurements showed that the ionization it produced is sensitive to draughts, and stable results could only be obtained by enclosing the apparatus in an air-tight box. The radioactive material being produced could have been either a gas or a vapour, so it was given the inclusive name 'emanation'. It lost its radioactivity after a time, and Rutherford measured the way in which it decreased as time went on. The curve that he obtained has a shape which is characteristic for the radioactive decay of any substance, whether the process is very fast or exceedingly slow. In this case the activity falls to half its first value in 54.5 seconds, to one quarter in 109 seconds, and to one eighth in 163.5 seconds: it is halved every 54.5 seconds, and thorium emanation thus has a characteristic 'half-life' of 54.5 seconds.

A young Englishman, Frederick Soddy, arrived at McGill in the summer of 1900. An Oxford chemistry graduate, he had applied unsuccessfully for a post at Toronto but obtained one at Montreal, and described his experience vividly:

> Rutherford and his radioactive emanations and active deposits got me before many weeks had elapsed and I abandoned all to follow him. For more than two years, scientific life became hectic to a degree rare in the lifetime of an individual, rare perhaps in the lifetime of an institution. The discovery that the emanations were Argon [family] gases, followed by that of Th-X as an intermediate product between Thorium and the emanation it produces, led rapidly to the complete interpretation of radioactivity as a natural process of spontaneous atomic disintegration and transmutation.
>
> ... The first magnetic deviation of the alpha rays by

Rutherford, and then later successful electrostatic devia-
tions, were also notable events. I recall seeing him dancing
like a dervish and emitting extraordinary imprecations, most
probably in the Maori tongue, having inadvertently taken
hold of the little deviation chamber before disconnecting the
high-voltage battery and, under the influence of a power
beyond his own, dashing it violently to the ground, so that
its beautifully and cunningly made canalization system was
strewn in ruins all over the floor.

Chance had set him on a course to collaborate with Rutherford in a successful attack on radioactivity, and later to make
another major contribution to the theory of the atom.

The nature of the beta rays soon became clear. Becquerel
and also Giesel showed in 1899 that they were electrons,
the same as Thomson's cathode rays, but with much higher
velocity. The alpha rays proved more difficult, although
a radium source of greater intensity was obtained from
France. The physics department's electromagnet, at full
power, produced a barely perceptible curvature; but with
the electrical department's largest dynamo the effect was
clear. Rutherford characteristically chanted 'Onward Chris-
tian soldiers'. The direction of curvature showed that the
alpha particles, unexpectedly, were positively charged. They
turned out to be travelling at about one tenth of the speed
of light, and to be very much more massive than electrons.
Rutherford, partly because of helium found in radioactive
minerals, guessed (correctly) that alpha particles are ions of
helium atoms (mass 4) and have a double positive charge. A
third kind of radiation produced by radioactive substances
is highly penetrating, but not deflected by a magnetic field.
These 'gamma' rays were first observed in France in 1900 by
P. Villard and eventually shown to be X-rays of extremely
short wavelength.

The complexity of the process of radioactive change rapidly became more obvious during this period (1900–3). In Germany, Professor Dorn at Halle had found that radium, like thorium, produced an 'emanation'. In London, Crookes appeared to have obtained a new radioactive material from previously purified uranium. In Paris (1901), Becquerel was puzzled. He had found that he could easily remove the radioactivity from his uranium by chemical purification, but somehow it always returned. Specimens of deactivated uranium tested after a year were again radioactive. Rutherford and Soddy found that more than half the radioactivity of thorium comes from a substance they called thorium x, which can be removed by purification. After a few weeks the thorium is found again to contain thorium x, and also the thorium emanation, which decays in the way that Rutherford had described. Soddy identified the thorium 'emanation' as a new inert gas of the argon group, which Ramsay had just discovered. The radium 'emanation', radon, is also an inert gas of this group, and with nearly the same atomic weight.

All the complications could be explained if the radioactivity of thorium or uranium was in each case the cumulative effect of a series of separate events or steps. At each stage an alpha particle or beta particle, or both, is or are expelled from the atom, leaving behind a new radioactive substance which may have a half-life measured in minutes, days, or many years.

In two scientific articles (1903), Rutherford and Soddy put forward this 'disintegration' theory, and in 1904 Rutherford described it at a meeting of the Royal Society in London. It was received cautiously because it was also a 'transmutation' theory. The appearance of argon-type atoms in the radioactive 'decay' sequence clearly seemed to imply the spontaneous breakdown of some of the heaviest types of atoms in the periodic table. Coming only a year or two after the electron was discovered, this underlined the need for a new model of the atom to replace the indestructible 'billiard ball' of the nineteenth century.

Another aspect of radioactivity which excited much interest was the large amount of energy released in the process. Rutherford's estimate of the high velocity of alpha particles led to a rough estimate that 1 gram of radium would produce a total of about 5 thousand million joules (energy) before its activity was exhausted, and at a rate of about 63,000 joules per year. Pierre Curie and Albert Leborde (1903) found that a sample of barium chloride containing radium chloride stayed about 1.5° warmer than pure barium chloride in identical surroundings. They estimated, from electrical measurements, that 1 gram of radium produces about 370 thousand joules per year.

These preliminary estimates did not agree too well, but they left no doubt that the energy available from radioactivity is very much greater than that from ordinary chemical change. One gram of radium releases thousands of millions of joules, but the complete burning of 1 gram of natural gas yields only about 50,000 joules.

In 1904 Rutherford and Soddy speculated boldly that:

> There is no reason to suppose that this enormous store of energy is possessed by the radio elements alone . . . The maintenance of solar energy . . . no longer presents any fundamental difficulty if the internal energy of the component elements is considered to be available, i.e., if processes of subatomic change are going on.

They identified many of the steps in the three main radioactive sequences from uranium via radium, from uranium via actinium, and from thorium, which all terminate in inactive lead atoms. Some of the elements involved have very long half-lives (for example, uranium, 4,510 million years), and the Yale scientist Bertram B. Boltwood (1870–1927) first suggested that the rocks of the earth's crust could be dated from their radioactivity and lead content. The high temperatures of the interior of the earth are also seen to be due to heating by radioactivity processes in the rocks.

In 1903 Soddy accepted an invitation to work with Ramsay in London for a year. Using very pure radium bromide they were able to isolate small amounts of a gas which formed within the radium salt after its recrystallization; and as Soddy had expected, on analysis it gave the full spectrum of helium. This was clear, direct evidence that atoms of one element can break down to yield atoms of another element, as he and Rutherford had envisaged in 1903.

In the meantime Rutherford had been investigating the mass and electric charge of the alpha particles from radium. From their deflection in magnetic and electric fields he was fairly certain that they had a mass of 4 and a charge of +2 (helium atoms which have lost two electrons), but to be certain he needed to be able to count the alpha particles as they were emitted. Attempts to do so using a scintillation method devised by Crookes were not at first successful. An interesting visitor to Rutherford's laboratory in 1905–6 was Otto Hahn (1879–1968) of Marburg, the future discoverer of nuclear fission. With a background in organic chemistry, he had spent the year 1904–5 in England with Ramsay to gain experience. It so happened that he was assigned to the task of separating radium from barium chloride and was able to identify a new radioactive substance (radio-thorium). He spent the following year at Montreal with Rutherford (and Boltwood) and discovered radio-actinium. He returned to Berlin having been set on the path to future fame, as had Soddy before him.

In 1907 a new stage in Rutherford's investigations of alpha particles and the structure of atoms began with his acceptance of an offer of a physics professorship in England, at Manchester University. Here he resumed work on the properties of alpha particles and atomic structure, again using the zinc sulphide screens of Crookes, which showed tiny, bright scintillations wherever a single alpha particle struck. His assistants were Hans Geiger (1882–1945) and a young fellow New Zealander, Ernest Marsden. In 1910 they discovered a remarkable effect:

> In the early days I had observed the scattering of alpha particles, and Dr Geiger in my laboratory had examined it in detail. He found in thin pieces of heavy metal that the scattering was usually small, of the order of one degree. One day Geiger came to me and said, 'Don't you think that young Marsden, whom I am training in radioactive methods, ought to begin a small research?' Now I had thought that too, so I said, 'Why not let him see if any alpha particles can be scattered through a large angle?' I may tell you in confidence that I did not believe they would be, since we knew that the alpha particle was a very fast massive particle, with a great deal of energy, and you could show that if the scattering was due to the accumulated effect of a number of small scatterings, the chance of an alpha particle's being scattered backwards was very small. Then I remember two or three days later Geiger coming to me in great excitement and saying, 'We have been able to get some of the alpha particles coming backwards'. . . . It was quite the most incredible event that has happened to me in my life. It was almost as incredible as if you fired a 15-inch shell at a piece of tissue paper and it came back and hit you.

On consideration I realised that this scattering backwards

must be the result of a single collision and when I made calculations it was impossible to get anything of that order of magnitude unless you took a system in which the greater part of the mass of the atom was concentrated in a minute nucleus.

(Ernest Rutherford)

Rutherford considered various explanations for the new result but, early in 1911, concluded that the atom consists of a very small nucleus which contains almost its entire mass and carries a number of positive electric charges. In orbits far out from the nucleus are electrons which each have a negative charge and are equal in number to the central positive charge. This system is mainly empty space. The backward scattering of some of the alpha particles results from rare close encounters with the tiny, massive nuclei of the metal atoms in the gold foil.

He described these conclusions in 1911 at the same Manchester Society to which Dalton had spoken of atomic weights a century before. A detailed account was published later the same year, with a study of the scattering process which gave results in broad agreement with the proposed structure.

One difficulty that did exist was that, according to accepted electromagnetic theory, the electrons orbiting round the nucleus should give off electromagnetic radiation, lose energy and spiral in to the nucleus. Niels Bohr solved this by applying quantum theory. Only orbits of certain energies are allowed, and only when an electron moves to a higher or lower orbit must a quantum of radiation be absorbed or emitted. Bohr's theory showed that when an electron in the atom jumps into an inner orbit (towards the nucleus) the quantum emitted is in the X-ray region, and if the wavelength could be measured the charge on the atomic nucleus could be calculated.

Henry Moseley, a young physicist at Manchester was then working on exact methods for measuring the wavelengths of X-rays. To test Bohr's theory he calculated the nuclear charge for each of a series of elements of medium atomic weight. His results, published in 1913, showed that the positive charge on each nucleus is a whole-number multiple of the negative electrical charge on an electron, which is exactly as expected. But the surprise finding of Moseley's research was that, in moving up the periodic table from low to high atomic weights, the charge on the nucleus increases by one unit at a time. The first element, hydrogen, has a nuclear charge of +1.00; the twentieth, calcium, has a charge of +20.00; the twenty-sixth, iron is +25.99; and the thirtieth, zinc, is +30.01. Thus the elements found on earth actually constitute a sequence in which the nuclear charge increases, with only a handful of gaps, from +1 to +92. According to Soddy:

> Moseley . . . called the roll of the elements, so that for the first time we could say definitely the number of possible elements between the beginning and the end, and the number that still remained to be found.

The nucleus contains virtually all the mass of an atom and as, for example, the atomic weight of calcium is 40.09 and its nuclear charge is +20.00, clearly the nucleus cannot simply be a lump of hydrogen nuclei which have a mass of 1.00 and a charge of +1.00. The first explanation was that in this case the nucleus must contain 40 protons and, mixed in with them, 20 practically weightless negative electrons, which reduce the nuclear charge to +20. This explanation sufficed for a while.

A second question worrying scientists concerned atomic weights. Many are very close to being whole numbers but some, like chlorine at 35.45, are not. Work by Soddy established that amongst the radioactive elements there are several with strong chemical similarities but different half-lives and atomic weights. He explained that thorium, mesothorium and thorium x are chemically identical but have atomic weights which differ from each other by four units (the mass of an alpha particle).

Soddy came to the conclusion that these should be considered the same element. Occupying the same slot in the periodic table, these were simply 'isotopes' of slightly different atomic weights. In 1913 his theory was confirmed; it was demonstrated that the chemical properties of an atom are determined by the 'skin' of outer electrons but the number and arrangement of these electrons in the electrically neutral state is controlled by the nuclear charge (atomic number). If an alpha particle is shot out of the nucleus it loses four units of mass and two positive charges. The atom therefore becomes chemically different and moves two places down in the table. Should the nucleus subsequently expel two electrons (beta particles) its mass will not change appreciably, but the charge on the nucleus will increase to the original value. The net result is a lighter isotope of the same element.

The start of World War I in August 1914 greatly reduced scientific research activity. In 1917 Rutherford discovered that alpha particles will penetrate the nitrogen nucleus and knock out a proton; but one of his closest collaborators, James Chadwick, was in Germany working with Geiger when war broke out, and spent four years in internment, whilst Moseley had his brains blown out by a Turkish sniper during the Gallipoli landings in 1915.

In the 1920s, top priority for Rutherford and his followers

became the structure of the nucleus. Together with two assistants, J. D. Cockcroft and E. T. S. Walton, he used a proton accelerator at half a million volts to bombard the light metal lithium with protons (hydrogen nuclei). This caused a nuclear reaction in which an atom of lithium (mass 7) and a proton (mass 1) formed two alpha particles (ionized helium atoms) with a total mass of 8.

But the actual (as opposed to nominal) masses of lithium and hydrogen are 7.016 and 1.008 respectively; a total of 8.024. The two alpha particles that result from the reaction were measured as having a total mass of 8.008, a mass of 0.016 has been converted into a large amount of kinetic energy, which agrees with the reaction $E = mc^2$. This was the first physical confirmation of Einstein's equation.

Rutherford speculated as early as 1920 that there might be a particle of the same mass as a proton but with no electric charge. He referred to it as the 'neutron' and pointed out that because of its lack of electrical charge it should easily be able to penetrate the atomic nucleus where a proton could not. It proved to be extremely elusive.

In a conversation with Ritchie Calder, a scientific journalist, Rutherford was asked how it would be possible to detect a particle with no electric charge. He replied:

You could still follow its movement through; it's as though [H. G.] Wells' invisible man were playing in a football match – you couldn't see him but you could follow his passage up the field by the players staggering out of his way as he charged them.

Despite this, the breakthrough came in a curiously round-about way. In 1930, Professor Walther Bothe and Becker in Germany bombarded boron and beryllium with alpha particles from polonium and found a radiation far more powerful than gamma rays. They concluded that this was gamma radiation of several million volts' energy. Interested by this, Jean-Frederic Joliot and Irene Curie followed the experiment up with a more powerful polonium source and found that the radiation caused very rapid motion in hydrogen nuclei in paraffin and cellophane; they concluded that the cause was photons of enormous energy. In fact, as Chadwick in Cambridge realized, they were watching the invisible man playing football. His explanation and experimental confirmation were published slightly less than a month after the Joliot-Curies' tentative but wrong account appeared, to their distinct irritation.

One day in October 1937, Rutherford went out into his garden in Cambridge to prune a tree. He fell and injured himself. The next day, after seeing his doctor, a strangulated hernia was diagnosed and he was taken to a local hospital for surgery. Although it was a simple enough operation, infection set in and he was dead within a week. His colleague James Jeans described his importance to science:

> Voltaire said once that Newton was more fortunate than any other scientist could ever be, since it could fall to only one man to discover the laws which governed the universe. Had he lived in a later age, he might have said something similar of Rutherford and the realm of the infinitely small; for Rutherford was the Newton of atomic physics.

Chadwick's discovery of the neutron gave physicists an entirely new tool with which to attack the nucleus of the atom. Bombardment with electrically charged particles had hitherto required enormously high levels of energy to overcome mutual electrical repulsion and had, despite talk in the popular press of 'splitting the atom', really only ever succeeded in knocking small fragments away from atomic nuclei. The neutron, on the other hand, carrying no electrical charge, would not be diverted from its course until it struck a nucleus. A chance finding in an Italian laboratory led to an even more surprising discovery.

In the spring of 1934, Enrico Fermi, a 33-year-old Italian nuclear physicist, was conducting a series of experiments in which he was irradiating elements in an attempt to induce artificial radiation. When he finally got to element 92, uranium, he observed a curious phenomenon. He had found that light elements generally transmuted to even lighter ones under bombardment by ejecting a proton or an alpha particle. But heavier nuclei apparently captured neutrons that hit them, thus gaining one more unit of atomic number, which would mean, in the case of uranium, that it was changing firstly into a heavier isotope, U239, and then, as it shed a beta particle, into element 93 – a substance that was not known to exist on earth. The products of Fermi's neutron bombardment of uranium certainly did not seem to behave like other known heavy elements – the result that might be expected – and he became more and more convinced that he was creating new, 'transuranic' elements.

Fermi's apparent discovery was naturally a cause of great excitement amongst physicists and chemists, and throughout the latter half of the 1930s they laboured to nail down what the products of the bombardment of uranium actually were. There was speculation that, in addition to element 93, uranium was giving birth to 94, 95 and even 96. Even those who questioned the likelihood of transuranic materials being produced were unable to provide an explanation of what was occurring; it was suggested, for example, the element 91, or protactinium, was being produced, but when this was tested by Otto

Hahn, who had discovered it in the first place, it was found not to be the case.

One dissenting voice was raised by a Hungarian chemist working in Germany, Ida Noddack. She suggested that by restricting their research to the rare earth and heavy elements which were supposed to be the most likely products of uranium bombardment, researchers were leaving huge areas unexplored. She thought that it was possible that the nuclei of heavy atoms broke into large fragments which would be isotopes of unrelated elements. Although this view had both logic and plausibility on its side, it was widely dismissed as being cranky and wrong.

But, in truth, Noddack was not far from the answer. Increasingly, experimenters were finding results that suggested that the products of uranium bombardment came from much further *down* the Periodic Table, rather than from the uranium end. Irene Curie tentatively suggested that one substance was 'like lanthanum' (element 57) without ever realizing the truth. Investigation of this possibility by Otto Hahn at the Kaiser Wilhelm Institute in Berlin led to a startling conclusion that Hahn felt violated all previous experimental evidence in nuclear physics; he believed that uranium under neutron bombardment had transmuted into two much lighter elements, barium and lanthanum.

So great were the misgivings of Hahn and his colleague Fritz Strassman that their report was couched only in the vaguest and most neutral turns. Even then, Hahn felt the need to discuss his findings with his old and valued colleague, Lise Meitner, who had by then fled from Nazi persecution to Stockholm. Just before Christmas 1938, Hahn wrote to Meitner, who was spending the holiday with her nephew Otto Frisch at a Swedish seaside village overlooking the Baltic. Frisch, another Jewish refugee, was then working with Niels Bohr in Denmark and was consequently thoroughly versed in Bohr's concept that the nucleus of an atom was similar in many respects to a droplet of water. As Meitner and her nephew discussed Hahn's letter and his finding that uranium nuclei were apparently breaking in two, Frisch recalled Bohr's droplet theory and understood how the process must work:

> A nucleus was not like a brittle solid that can be cleaved or broken . . . a nucleus was much more like a liquid drop. Perhaps a drop could divide itself into two smaller drops in a more gradual manner, by first becoming elongated, then constricted, and finally being torn rather than broken in two? We knew that there were strong forces that would resist such a process, just as the surface tension of an ordinary liquid drop tends to resist its division into two smaller ones. But the nuclei differed from ordinary drops in one important way: they were electrically charged, and that was known to counteract surface tension.
>
> . . . so the uranium nucleus might indeed resemble a very wobbly, unstable drop, ready to divide itself at the slightest provocation, such as the impact of a single neutron.

Frisch and Meitner also worked out that, as they separated, the two drops would acquire a very high speed and thus a large energy. Where would this have come from? Meitner calculated that about one fifth of the mass of a proton would be lost during the division and, using Einstein's formula for the conversion of mass into energy, $E = mc^2$, found that it seemed to fit. Excited by their discovery, Frisch returned to Copenhagen to tell Bohr.

2

The Race for the Bomb

The period between the two world wars was one of great political instability and uncertainty in Europe. World War I had been launched, essentially, by the German Kaiser Wilhelm II out of his frustration that newly unified Germany was unable to achieve the 'parity of esteem' with the other great European powers – by which were meant Russia, France and Britain – that he felt had been earned by its newly achieved industrial and military muscle. The international squabbles that took place in the Balkans in the summer of 1914 culminated, as a result of the confused alliance system of the time, in a general descent into a war in which Germany and the Austro-Hungarian Empire faced off against Russia, Britain and France. Had the war followed the traditional pattern of the previous century or so, a decision would have been swift; one can conjecture that a series of manoeuvres and skirmish battles might have culminated in one or more decisive engagements during which the armies of one side would have been broken and destroyed, leaving a triumphant victor to dictate peace terms. But this was not the case; as every student of history knows, the German invasion of Belgium and France became bogged down into a series of static holding actions as each side sought to achieve a breakthrough. After a few months, this had developed into bitter trench warfare, which was to endure for the next four years and witness the destruction of a significant proportion of the young men of that generation.

In August 1914, people reacted in different ways to the outbreak of war; many people at that time, before wars had become the all-consuming slaughter that we now know them to be, were enthusiastic in general terms, seeing war between states as an almost academic test of national virility. Adolf Hitler, a young aimless drifter making a bare living in the south German city of Munich by selling postcards and architectural drawings, was overjoyed:

> For me these hours came as a deliverance from the distress
> that had weighed upon me during the days of my youth . . .
> I sank down on my knees to thank heaven for the favour of
> having been permitted to live in such a time.

And, despite spending the better part of the next four years as a front-line soldier, close to the action, he never lost his enthusiasm for destruction. But most people who took part in the fighting, and those who lost members of their family and close friends, were horrified by the slaughter.

Amongst a number of reasons for the sheer nastiness of World War I was that it was the first time in which the cutting edge of human technology, applied to weapons of destruction, had been used on a massive scale. The late nineteenth and early twentieth centuries had seen revolutionary advances in a broad spectrum of fields; scientists and engineers were producing bold conceptual leaps forward whilst industrialists and manufacturers massively increased the numbers in which new products could be made. Along with the socially useful products of the industrial revolution, like the railways, steamships and the internal combustion engine, came rifled breech-loading artillery, submarines, machine guns and a host of other implements to multiply the destructive power of one set of combatants over another. By the time World War I had broken out, all the participants had sufficient modern weaponry to ensure that none of them could achieve decisive superiority over the others without inflicting considerable 'attrition' on a scale not really considered before then; as a result, scientists were called upon to see how they could contribute.

Another novel feature of World War I was the use of weapons of mass destruction. Indiscriminate aerial bombing of civilian targets was practised for the first time by both sets of combatants; and perhaps more significantly, Germany pioneered the employment of the first terror weapon, poisonous chlorine gas, against French and British troops on the Western front.

The use of gas, subsequently adopted with enthusiasm by Britain and France, represented an entirely new category of warfare, which could, if properly used, exert a decisive and strategic influence on the course of a battle by the simple expedient of killing and disabling large numbers of the enemy at a given point. In the words of one of the German pioneers of gas warfare, the chemist Fritz Haber, it represented 'a higher form of killing'.

Although gas was responsible for death and injury to thousands during the war, and although scientists developed more efficient and effective gases to use, in actual fact it was only occasionally responsible for tactical successes at the front, and never for any decisive strategic success. Gas never really was properly used, largely because the technological means did not exist to deliver it in such a way as to nullify the various countermeasures that were available. What it did do was raise the possibility of new categories of weapon, hitherto unthought of, as a means of winning wars; and alert those involved in the waging of wars that such weapons might be discovered.

The crises that afflicted Europe in the years after World War One were largely the result of the Allies' victory in it. The Central Powers – Germany and Austria-Hungary – were forced to concede defeat in the autumn of 1918 as a result of a combination of economic and political collapse on the 'home front' and increasing military pressure on the Western front. But although German military resistance was in the process of crumbling when the government sued for peace, the German army had certainly not been comprehensively beaten; indeed, it is not inconceivable that it might have been able to rally, at least temporarily, and continue the fight for a few more months. For the front-line soldiers of Germany, it seemed that they had been 'stabbed in the back' by politicians and war profiteers at home. One particular soldier, Corporal Hitler of the 16th Bavarian Reserve Infantry Regiment, was unable at first to comprehend what had happened – the psychological shock of the armistice caused a relapse into the blindness from which he had been suffering, having been gassed a few months before – but German defeat sparked in him a determination to get back at the 'Social-Democrats, Bolsheviks and Jews' who had betrayed the soldiers at the front.

Although Hitler's response to Germany's defeat – leading the Nazi Party to power – was somewhat singular to say the least, nevertheless, he personified in an extreme way the international politics of Europe in the 1920s and 1930s. This was to achieve a resolution of the issues that the abrupt end to World War I had left incomplete. Part of Hitler's solution, after he took power in Germany in January 1933, involved an initially stealthy rearmament programme; another very significant element was the persecution of Germany's Jewish population.

One of the first measures that Hitler's government introduced was a decree forbidding 'non-Aryans' from remaining in the German civil service. As all the universities and many research establishments in Germany were state institutions, this had the immediate effect of sacking the majority of working Jewish scientists in the country. These scientists in fact made up a quarter of German physicists and included eleven people who had won or were subsequently to win the Nobel prize. In the new anti-Semitic climate of Germany, those who lost their jobs in this way were unlikely to be able to gain employment elsewhere, and it began to be recognized that to continue to work as scientists, they would need to leave the country. The young Austrian Jew Otto Frisch was working in Hamburg in collaboration with Otto Stern, another Austrian-born theoretical physicist of Jewish background:

It soon became clear that [Hitler's] anti-Semitism was not just talk, and when his racial laws were passed, Stern was quite shocked to find that I was of Jewish origin, just as he was himself and another two of his four collaborators. He would have to leave and the three of us as well, only one of his outfit – Friedrich Knauer – being Aryan and able to remain in a university post. Actually the university in Hamburg – with the traditions of a free Hansa city – was very reluctant to put the racial laws into effect, and I wasn't sacked until several months after the other universities had toed the line. At first I still hoped that I might be able to take up a fellowship which the Rockefeller Foundation has awarded me (at Stern's instigation) to enable me to work in Rome for a year, an opportunity I had very much looked forward to . . . But the fellowship was conditional on my having a permanent post to go back to; when Hitler's laws came into effect the Rockefeller Foundation regretfully informed me that under those circumstances they could not offer me the fellowship any longer.

The random lawlessness of Nazism meant that nobody was really safe:

Disturbing rumours were rife. Some of my Jewish friends had warned me not to be out at night because Jews had been beaten up in the dark.

Nazi persecution prompted many of its victims into action. Frisch managed to obtain a job at London University; but some of the more prominent refugees were in a position to organize help for others as well as themselves. Leo Szilard, the Hungarian physicist, approached Sir William Beveridge, the director of the London School of Economics, to explain the situation and ask for aid. To his credit, Beveridge was able to persuade Ernest Rutherford in Cambridge to join him in organizing an 'Academic Assistance Council' whose purpose was to find jobs for the German Jewish refugees. Largely funded by American contributions, an exodus of some of the finest minds in science and the arts took place from Germany whilst the Nazi leaders crowed at their supposed triumphs over the 'World Jewish Conspiracy'.

A German chemist, Kurt Mendelssohn, remembered:

When I woke up the sun was shining in my face. I had slept deeply, soundly and long – for the first time in many weeks . . . I had arrived in London and gone to bed without fear that at 3 a.m. a car with a couple of SA men would draw up and take me away.

The list of those who left Germany for the safety of the democracies included Albert Einstein, Hans Bethe, Edward Teller, Lise Meitner, James Franck, Max Born and hundreds of others; it is a kind of monument to the stupidity of anti-Semitism.

Thus it was that some six and a half years after the first Nazi anti-Semitic laws were passed, on 1 September 1939, when the tanks of Hitler's *Wehrmacht* stormed across the border into neighbouring Poland, German physics was in a considerably weakened state. Hahn's work at the Kaiser Wilhelm Institute had shown that the nuclear fission of uranium, with its consequent release of energy, was a fact, and from there it was not difficult to deduce, as many had, that with a sufficiently large piece of uranium it might be possible to produce a chain reaction with an enormous release of energy. Although Bohr at this stage thought that a bomb would not be possible (and within the terms he was using he was right), others were not so sure. Leo Szilard, now in the United States, who had conceived the idea of a chain reaction some years before, wrote to a friend that the discovery might:

lead to large-scale production of energy and radioactive elements, unfortunately also perhaps to atomic bombs. This new discovery revives all the hopes and fears in this respect which I had in 1934 and 1935, and which I have as good as abandoned in the course of the last two years.

Together with Enrico Fermi, who had been forced to leave

Italy after winning the Nobel prize because his wife was Jewish, and Walter Zinn, one of Fermi's senior collaborators, Szilard hired the necessary equipment to bombard natural uranium with neutrons. Szilard and Fermi wanted to see how many neutrons were emitted when uranium was itself bombarded with them; these newly emitted neutrons would show as flashes on a television screen:

> We turned the switch and we saw the flashes. We watched for a while and then we turned off the machine and went home. That night, there was little doubt in my mind the world was headed for grief.

Others were thinking on the same lines. The Polish scientist Joseph Rotblat, then in Warsaw, had also heard of Hahn's discovery of fission:

> Because of the work I had been doing it did not take me long after a simple experiment to conclude that a divergent chain reaction with a vast release of energy was possible. The logical sequel was that if this energy were released in a very short time it would result in an explosion of unprecedented power.

Hahn too had thought through the consequences of his discovery, but, unhappy with the thought that the Nazis might develop a weapon of unparalleled power, he decided to keep his ideas to himself for the time being. And it was here that the idiocy of the Nazi anti-Semitic policy was most evident; as a result of their racist persecution, the 'Third Reich' had voluntarily excluded many of the scientists who might have been able to follow up Hahn's work independently of him. To be sure, there were still a number of gifted scientists who had not been forced to emigrate, but the scientific community in Germany was significantly smaller, and thus significantly less able to advance in isolation, than it had been before Hitler came to power. Even so, without Hahn's direct assistance, two groups of German scientists independently began work on the potentialities of uranium energy during 1939. One group, under Professor Abraham Esau, discussed with the Reich Ministry of Education how a 'uranium burner' might be constructed, and began preparations for obtaining stocks of uranium from within Germany. The second group, lead by Professor Paul Harteck of Hamburg, wrote to the German War Office:

> We take the liberty of calling to your attention the newest development in nuclear physics, which, in our opinion, will probably make it possible to produce an explosive many orders of magnitude more powerful than the conventional ones.

A participant of the conference with Professor Esau was Hahn's deputy, Josef Mattauch. On his return to the Kaiser Wilhelm Institute he met two theoretical physicists from the institute who had been looking at the release of energy in fission. Frisch in Denmark had calculated that the energy released by one atom fissioning would be enough to make a visible grain of sand jump visibly (which is impressive when one considers that there are about 2,500,000,000,000,000,000,000 atoms in such a grain of sand). Siegfried Flugge, one of the physicists, calculated:

> One cubic metre of consolidated uranium-oxide powder weighs 4.2 tons and contains 3,000 million-million-million-million molecules, or three times as many uranium atoms.

As each atom liberates about 180 million electron-volts (about three ten-thousandths of an erg), in other words three million-millionths of a kilogram metre, a total energy of 27,000 million-million kilogram metres would be liberated. That means that one cubic metre of uranium-oxide would be sufficient to lift a cubic-kilometre of water (total weight: 10 million-million kilograms) twenty seven kilometres into the air!

The letter from Harteck to the War Office stirred them sufficiently to establish an office to examine the possibilities of nuclear fission. By the time the war started, a small group of eminent German scientists was in the process of being mobilized.

The outbreak of war in Europe seems to have acted as a spur to others as well. The commandant of the Japanese air force research institute ordered a report to be drawn up into the possibilities of a nuclear fission bomb in early 1940, whilst Soviet scientists also continued with their research through that period. But a strange silence fell over the world's scientific community as the war in Europe got under way; although nuclear fission was one of the more exciting discoveries in physics in recent years, very little research was published, as scientists digested its implications.

The first free-world scientists to attempt to alert the authorities to the possibilities of nuclear fission were Fermi and Szilard, who made independent approaches to the US government. In March 1939, Enrico Fermi spoke to officers of the US armed forces in Washington DC, outlining the future possibilities for uranium research; but his knowledge was, at this early stage, so sketchy that they were unable to make any particular commitment to him. In any case, he was slightly put off on his arrival at the Navy Department to overhear an officer telling his official host that 'There's a wop outside.'

Characteristically, Szilard took a somewhat more flamboyant approach to the problem. He had continued his work with Fermi, examining whether it would be possible to moderate the speed of fast neutrons using graphite, and come to the disturbing conclusion that it would. He decided to share his results with two Hungarian friends, both of whom were refugees from central European Fascism: Eugene Wigner and Edward Teller. In July 1939 they met in New York and discussed their options. Between them they decided that developments were so important that they were obliged to enlist the help of the government.

At the same time, the three Hungarians became concerned at the notion that Nazi Germany might be able to obtain supplies of uranium ore from the Congo, then ruled by Belgium. Szilard knew that his friend Albert Einstein was an acquaintance of the queen of Belgium and thought that he might be persuaded to write to her and warn of the possible danger.

Szilard and Wigner discovered that Einstein was spending the summer on Long Island, and made an appointment to call on him there. The two Hungarians arrived on Sunday 16 July, reaching the house during the early afternoon. Einstein was, even then, regarded as perhaps the most important scientific theoretician since Newton, and an image has been passed down to us of a frail, slightly unkempt, intellectual. The truth could not have been more different, according to the British scientific journalist, C. P. Snow:

At close quarters, Einstein's head was as I had imagined it: magnificent with a humanising touch of the comic. Great furrowed forehead; aureole of white hair; enormous bulging chocolate eyes. I can't guess what I should have expected from such a face if I hadn't known.

A shrewd Swiss once said it had the brightness of a good artisan's countenance, that he looked like a reliable old fashioned watchmaker in a small town who perhaps collected butterflies on a Sunday.

What did surprise me was his physique. He . . . was wearing nothing but a pair of shorts. It was a massive body, very heavily muscled: he was running to fat round the midriff and the upper arms, rather like a footballer in middle-age, but he was still an unusually strong man. He was cordial, simple, utterly unshy.

Szilard explained to him his ideas about the possibilities of a chain reaction. Einstein expostulated: 'I never thought of that!', and listened intently, quickly agreeing to help in any way he could. He drafted a letter to the Belgian government, which the Hungarians took away to have translated and typed. At this point fate took a hand; a friend of Szilard's discussed the matter with Dr Alexander Sachs, a Russian-born biologist and economist, who convinced Szilard that he should act as an intermediary to President Franklin Roosevelt himself. This was a possibility because of Sachs' support for the administration over a long period, which included speech writing for the president in his first administration, but he insisted that the text of the message needed revision. As a result, Szilard returned to Long Island, this time with Edward Teller as his driver, to confer with Einstein. The letter, in its final form, was given to Sachs to pass to the president on 15 August 1939:

Albert Einstein
Old Grove Road
Nassau Point
Peconic, Long island
August 2nd, 1939

F. D. Roosevelt
President of the United States,
White House
Washington, D. C.

Sir:

Some recent work by E. Fermi and L. Szilard, which has been transmitted to me in manuscript, leads me to expect that the element uranium may be turned into a new and important source of energy in the immediate future. Certain aspects of the situation which has arisen seem to call for watchfulness and, if necessary, quick action on the part of the Administration. I believe therefore that it is my duty to bring to your attention the following facts and recommendations:

In the course of the last four months it has been made probable – through the work of Joliot in France as well as Fermi and Szilard in America – that it may become possible to set up a nuclear chain reaction in a large mass of uranium, by which vast amounts of power and large quantities of new radium-like elements would be generated. Now it appears almost certain that this could be achieved in the immediate future.

This new phenomenon would also lead to the construction of bombs, and it is conceivable – though much less certain – that extremely powerful bombs of a new type may thus be constructed. A single bomb of this type, carried by a boat and exploded in a port, might very well destroy the whole port together with some of the surrounding territory.

However, such bombs might very well prove to be too heavy for transportation by air.

The United States has only very poor ores of uranium in moderate quantities. There is some good ore in Canada and the former Czechoslovakia while the most important source of uranium is Belgian Congo.

In view of this situation you may think it desirable to have some permanent contact maintained between the Administration and the group of physicists working on chain reactions in America. One possible way of achieving this might be for you to entrust with this task a person who has your confidence and who could perhaps serve in an inofficial capacity. His task might comprise the following:

a) to approach Government Departments, keep them informed of the further development, and put forward recommendations for Government action, giving particular attention to the problem of securing a supply of uranium ore for the United States;

b) to speed up the experimental work, which is at present being carried on within the limits of the budgets of University laboratories, by providing funds, if such funds be required, through his contacts with private persons who are willing to make contributions for this cause, and perhaps also by obtaining the co-operation of industrial laboratories which have the necessary equipment.

I understand that Germany has actually stopped the sale of uranium from the Czechoslovakian mines which she has taken over. That she should have taken such early action might perhaps be understood on the ground that the son of the German under-secretary of State, von Weizsacker, is attached to the Kaiser-Wilhelm-Institut in Berlin where some of the American work on uranium is now being repeated.

Yours very truly,

(*Albert Einstein*)

Sachs was unable to see Roosevelt before 11 October 1939, ten weeks after the letter was written, but when he did talk to him, the president was impressed by what he heard. Roosevelt passed the letter to his private secretary, telling him that 'This needs action.'

Although it has assumed almost legendary status, Einstein's letter to Roosevelt did no more than provoke the formation of a committee under Dr Lyman J. Briggs to examine the issue. The first meeting of the 'Advisory Committee on Uranium' was on 21 October Washington DC. Participants included Briggs, his assistant, Sachs, Szilard, Teller, Wigner, Richard Roberts (an American nuclear physicist) and representatives of the army and navy. Although a small amount of money was eventually authorized to allow research to continue, the meeting did not achieve a great deal – after all, in October 1939, the United States was still more than two years away from being formally committed to the war and, although there was a certain sense of urgency, it was not yet the acute fear that would develop later.

By contrast, Great Britain had formally declared war on the Third Reich on 3 September 1939 and the scientific community was being galvanized into action. By coincidence, C. P. Snow, editor of the journal *Discovery*, chose that month to feature the possibilities of nuclear chain reactions in his editorial:

Some physicists think that, within a few months, science will have produced for military use an explosive a million times more violent than dynamite. It is no secret; laboratories in the United States, Germany, France and England have been working on it feverishly since the Spring. It may not come off. The most competent opinion is divided upon whether the idea is practicable. If it is, science for the first time will at one bound have altered the scope of warfare. The power of most scientific weapons has been consistently exaggerated; but it would be difficult to exaggerate this.

So there are two questions. *Will* it come off? How will the world be affected if it does?

As to the practicability, most of our opinions are worth little. The most eminent physicist with whom I have discussed it thinks it improbable; I have talked to others who think it as good as done. In America, as soon as the possibility came to light, it seemed so urgent that a representative of the physicists telephoned the White House and arranged an interview with the President. That was about three months ago. And it is in America where the thing will in all probability be done, if it is done at all.

The principle is fairly simple . . . Briefly it is this: a slow neutron knocks a uranium nucleus into two approximately equal pieces, and two or more *faster* neutrons are discharged at the same time. These faster neutrons go on to disintegrate other uranium nuclei, and the process is self-accelerating. It is the old dream of the release of intra-atomic energy, suddenly made actual at a time when most scientists had long discarded it; energy is *gained* by the trigger action of the first neutrons.

The idea of the uranium bomb is to disintegrate in this manner an entire lump of uranium. As I have said, many physicists of sound judgement consider that the technical difficulties have already been removed; but their critics ask – if this scheme were really workable, why have not the great uranium mines (the biggest are in Canada and the Congo) blown themselves up long ago? The percentage of uranium is very high: and there are always enough neutrons about to set such a trigger action going.

Well, in such a scientific controversy, with some of the ablest physicists in the world on each side, it would be presumptuous to intrude. But on the result there may depend a good many lives, and perhaps more than that.

For what will happen, if a new means of destruction, far more effective than any now existing, comes into our hands? I think most of us, certainly those working day and night this summer upon the problem in New York, are pessimistic about the result. We have seen too much of human selfishness and frailty to pretend that men can be trusted with a new weapon of gigantic power. Most scientists are by temperament fairly hopeful and simple minded about political things: but in the last eight years that hope has been drained away. In our time, at least, life has been impoverished, and not enriched, by the invention of flight. We cannot delude ourselves that this new invention will be better used.

Yet it must be made, if it really is a physical possibility. If it is not made in America this year, it may be next year in Germany. There is no ethical problem; if the invention is not prevented by physical laws, it will certainly be carried out somewhere in the world. It is better, at any rate, that America should have six months' start.

But again, we must not pretend. Such an invention will never be kept secret; the physical principles are too obvious, and within a year every big laboratory on earth would have come to the same result. For a short time, perhaps, the US Government may have this power entrusted to it; but soon after it will be in less civilised hands.

The Editor

Snow was, in fact, being unduly optimistic about the state

of uranium fission research in the US and pessimistic about the speed at which Germany and other interested parties would be able to follow the work. Although a fission explosion was a recognized theoretical possibility, it was still not clear how it might be practically achieved, but work which took place in England during the first year of the war was to point the way. It had been recognized since the mid-1930s that uranium consisted of two isotopes, one of atomic weight 238 and one of 235. U235 actually comprised about 0.7 per cent of any given sample of uranium but would, it was found, fission when it absorbed any neutron at all. U238 will only fission on absorbing a high-energy fast neutron and, because of the proportions of the two isotopes in any given sample of natural uranium, a gigantic amount would be needed before there were sufficient U235 nuclei to ensure a chain reaction (calculations indicated that it would be of the order of fifty tons or thereabouts – certainly much too much to be carried in an aircraft). In any case, the Danish physicist Niels Bohr, by then regarded as Rutherford's successor as the world's leading nuclear theorist, argued that a chain reaction of this sort would only grow at a moderate rate and the material would heat up, melt and partially evaporate before a violent explosion could take place. But rather than blindly accepting this, Otto Frisch, the young Austrian Jewish refugee who was now working at Birmingham University, fell to pondering what might happen if it was possible to separate the U235 isotope in a pure form. In the early spring of 1940, Frisch had some disturbing ideas:

I wondered . . . if one could . . . produce enough uranium-235 to make a truly explosive chain reaction possible, not dependent on slow neutrons. How much of the isotope would be needed? I used a formula derived by the French

theoretician Francis Perrin and refined by [Frisch's co-worker
Rudolph] Peierls to get an estimate. Of course I didn't
know how strongly fission neutrons would react with
uranium-235, but a plausible estimate gave me a figure
for the required amount of uranium-235. To my amazement
it was very much smaller than I had expected; it was not a
matter of tons, but something like a pound or two.

Of course I discussed the result with Peierls at once. I
had worked out the possible efficiency of my separation
system with the help of Clusius's formula, and we came
to the conclusion that with something like a hundred
thousand similar separation tubes one might produce a
pound of reasonably pure uranium-235 in a modest time,
measured in weeks. At that point we stared at each
other and realised an atomic bomb might after all be
possible.

They took their findings to their department head, Mark
Oliphant, an Australian, who told them to report the matter
to Sir Henry Tizard, who was then running a committee
advising the government on scientific problems concerned
with warfare. Tizard took the report seriously enough to
form yet another committee, this time to examine and
analyse Frisch and Peierls' results. The MAUD Committee
sat for nearly a year as the scientists in Britain attempted
to work out an effective means to separate physically the
two isotopes of uranium. But, of course, the British-based
scientists were by no means the only ones to be examining
the possibilities of a uranium bomb.

The German War Office, as we have seen, was interested
in the possibility of constructing uranium weapons or, at
least, uranium 'engines' from early on. By the summer of
1940, work had begun on a laboratory to be known as the
'Virus House' (a name designed to ward off the curious) in

the grounds of the Kaiser Wilhelm Institute. There the mathematical physicist Werner Heisenberg and his colleague Carl-Friedrich von Weiszacker intended to build a sub-critical reactor to measure neutron multiplication. This was to be done in a pit under the building in which they planned to use 'natural' uranium oxide with a shield of water. By December 1940 they had run the first experiment and it had not worked – ordinary hydrogen, as present in water, did not prove effective. Walther Bothe then looked at graphite and 'heavy' water as potential moderators and made the mistake that was to prevent the German uranium project from getting anywhere near constructing a bomb; he used contaminated graphite and got an incorrect reading. As a result, the German researchers discarded graphite and committed themselves to heavy water to moderate their reactions. Heavy water – in which the hydrogen component is from the heavier deuterium isotope of hydrogen – was an extremely rare commodity, only manufactured at a hydroelectric plant in Vemork in the Telemark region of Norway, then, of course, under German control.

Towards the end of 1940, Otto Frisch had moved to Liverpool University to work with Joseph Rotblat under James Chadwick. There Frisch discovered that his own preferred method of Clusius isotope separation would not work, but was reassured by Peierls, working in co-operation with yet another refugee from Nazi Germany, Franz Simon, that a porous barrier, although more complicated, certainly would. While this work continued, American physicists refined Frisch and Peierls' calculation of the critical mass and reached a figure slightly larger, though of a similar order of magnitude. They informed Chadwick that they believed a critical mass of U235 to be about eighteen pounds untamped, or about half that with a heavy tamper (a tamper is a heavy shield which reflects a proportion of escaping neutrons back into the mass of U235). Chadwick was horrified, as he described in 1969:

> I remember the spring of 1941 to this day. I realised then that a nuclear bomb was not only possible – it was inevitable. Sooner or later these ideas could not be peculiar to us. Everybody would think about them before long, and some country would put them into action . . . I had many sleepless nights. But I did realise how very very serious it could be. And I had then to start taking sleeping pills. It was the only remedy. I've never stopped since then. It's 28 years, and I don't think I've missed a single night in all those 28 years.

Although formally neutral in the war between Britain and Germany, it was obvious in 1940 that, despite the activities of isolationist politicians, the United States clearly favoured Britain. The British prime minister, Winston Churchill, who had taken office after the German invasion of France and the Low Countries in May, could see that there was no prospect of British victory without the help – and indeed hopefully the direct involvement – of the United States. In consequence he had initiated secret personal contacts with President Roosevelt to plead Britain's case and ordered Sir Henry Tizard to share Britain's most advanced technological secrets with American scientists as a *quid pro quo*. In the late summer of 1940, Tizard took a small delegation of technical experts, together with examples of their work. By far the most important item was the 'cavity magnetron', developed in Oliphant's Birmingham laboratory; this was a high-powered microwave generator able to enhance massively the capabilities of aircraft detection radars.

Tizard's mission did not include nuclear scientists at this stage, but it established a principle of technological exchange which was to endure through the atomic bomb project. The MAUD Committee finally reported in July 1941, concluding that:

> i. The committee considers that the scheme for a uranium bomb is practicable and likely to lead to decisive results in the war.
> ii. It recommends that this work continue on the highest priority and on the increasing scale necessary to obtain the weapon in the shortest possible time.
> iii. That the present collaboration with America should be continued and extended especially in the region of experimental work.

Elsewhere the report had decided that:

> We have now reached the conclusion that it will be possible to make an effective uranium bomb which, containing some 25lb of active material, would be equivalent as regards destructive effect to 1,800 tons of TNT and would also release large quantities of radioactive substances.

The report was discreetly circulated amongst the scientific establishment of the US to a mixed reception; although the scientists working for the British government were now convinced that a uranium bomb was feasible, their American counterparts remained divided. Lyman Briggs' 'Uranium Committee' was careful to commit itself to nothing more than a hope that useful power, perhaps for submarine propulsion, might be obtained from fission.

One American who was prepared to exert himself, however, was Dr Vannevar Bush, a New Englander and former dean of the engineering faculty at the Massachusetts Institute of Technology. Bush persuaded President Roosevelt, in the summer of 1940, that Roosevelt needed a committee to advise him on defence science, and that Bush was the man to head it for him. Roosevelt agreed and Bush was nominated to chair the National Defense Research Committee (NDRC) becoming the 'virtual czar of American defence science'. In comparison to Briggs, Bush, who was a mathematician and electrical engineer by training, was 'far more adaptable, determined, and not too timid to ask for the huge sums of money needed for the experimental development of uranium'. Bush recognized that the state of uranium research needed monitoring and some resolution had to be made out of the conflicting optimism of the Briggs and MAUD camps (the findings and minutes of MAUD meetings were circulated in the US before the report was completed). He appointed the professor of physics at Chicago University, Arthur Compton, to complete a review of progress. Compton was more pessimistic than the British but, even so, felt that uranium was worth pursuing in the long term:

> It would seem to us unlikely that the use of nuclear fission can become of military importance within less than two years . . . If, however the chain reaction can be produced and controlled, it may rapidly become a determining factor in warfare.

Despite this, doubts remained, and Bush diverted much of his attention to establishing a new 'Office of Scientific Research and Development' (OSRD) with himself as director. Through the late summer of 1941, even though more of the United States' most important scientists were accepting fission as an area worth researching on a large scale, no progress was made. It was only when the MAUD report from Britain was formally transmitted to Bush, in his new appointment, in October that he was able to present it directly to the president.

Franklin Roosevelt was no scientist but he was quick to grasp the essentials of the presentation that Bush made. His immediate decision was to reserve the essential task of nuclear policy making to a small group which included himself, Bush, James Conant (who had taken over from Bush as head of the NDRC), Vice-President Henry Wallace, Secretary of War Henry Stimson and Army Chief of Staff George Marshall. But he was unwilling to commit funds and authorize full-scale research until independent checks had been made on the British conclusions. These were to follow the next month in the shape of a National Academy of Science (NAS) review that Bush submitted to the president.

Bush received the NAS review back from Roosevelt on 19 January 1942. Attached was a short note which read:

V. B.
OK – returned – I think you had best keep this in your own safe.

FDR

This was, in effect, the authorization to attempt to build the bomb that would destroy Hiroshima.

3

The New World

On the evening of Sunday 7 December 1941, Winston Churchill was dining with the American ambassador, John Winant, and Averell Harriman, at Chequers, the British prime minister's official country residence just north of London. Churchill switched on his wireless set shortly after the nine o'clock news had started, and they heard a few lines concerning a Japanese attack on American shipping in Hawaii and against British vessels in the Dutch East Indies. Churchill immediately put through a telephone call to President Roosevelt in Washington; he confirmed the news. Imperial Japanese forces had attacked Pearl Harbor, and a significant proportion of the US Pacific Fleet had been damaged or sunk. Although the outbreak of hostilities had, to some extent, been anticipated, the attack on Pearl Harbor took the two great leaders by surprise. But if Roosevelt was understandably shocked and angered by the treachery of the Japanese attack – the Japanese were still ostensibly negotiating with the US – for Churchill the prevailing emotion was of profound relief.

No American will think it wrong of me if I proclaim that to have the United States at our side was to me the greatest joy. I could not foretell the course of events. I do not pretend to have measured accurately the martial might of Japan, but now at this very moment I knew the United States was in the war, up to the neck and in to the death. So we had won after all! Yes, after Dunkirk; after the fall of France; after the horrible episode of Oran; after the threat of invasion when, apart from the Air and the Navy we were almost an unarmed people; after the deadly struggle of the U-boat war – the first battle of the Atlantic, gained by a hand's-breadth; after seventeen months of lonely fighting and nineteen months of my responsibility in dire stress. We had won the war. England would live; Britain would live; the Commonwealth of Nations and the Empire would live. How long the war would last or in what fashion it would end no man could tell, nor did I at this moment care. Once again in our long Island history we should emerge, however mauled and mutilated, safe and victorious. We should not be wiped out. Our history would not come to an end. We might not even have to die as individuals. Hitler's fate was sealed. Mussolini's fate was sealed. As for the Japanese, they would be ground to powder. All the rest was merely the proper application of overwhelming force. The British Empire, the Soviet Union, and now the United States, bound together with every scrap of their life and strength, were, according to my lights, twice or even thrice the force of their antagonists. No doubt it would take a long time. I expected terrible forfeits in the East; but all this would be merely a passing phase. United we could subdue everybody else in the world. Many disasters, immeasurable cost and tribulation lay ahead, but there was no more doubt about the end.

Silly people, and there were many, not only in enemy

countries, might discount the force of the United States . . . But I had studied the American Civil War, fought to the last desperate inch. American blood flowed in my veins. I thought of a remark which Edward Grey had made to me more than thirty years before – that the United States is like 'a gigantic boiler. Once the fire is lighted under it there is no limit to the power it can generate'. Being saturated and satiated with emotion and sensation, I went to bed and slept the sleep of the saved and thankful.

Churchill's evident relief was understandable but, in some respects, Pearl Harbor put paid to Britain's hopes of being a full partner with the United States in the development of the atom bomb. Although, in December 1941, Britain appeared to have a lead over the United States in terms of bomb research, this was actually an illusion. The British effort (which, in any case, was to a great extent in the hands of refugees) was driven by the fierce imperatives of war, a 'super-weapon' like the atom bomb could be Britain's salvation and there was no time for collateral theoretical work such as could be, and was being, conducted by scientists in the US. But the resources to follow through the research and construct a bomb were not available in Britain, particularly at a time when a significant proportion of incoming supplies were being sent to the bottom of the Atlantic by U-boats, and when the *Luftwaffe* were regularly bombing Britain's main industrial centres. Britain, the bulwark of democracy against the threat of Nazism, was so preoccupied by the war that, as the British government dithered over whether to share research formally and in full, the lead in the race to build nuclear weaponry passed irrevocably to the United States.

By the beginning of 1942 the theoretical position was clear to those who were privy to the secrets. If sufficient U235 could be separated from natural uranium ores then a bomb could be assembled with a critical mass of practical size. The difficulties remaining related to calculating a precise figure for a critical mass; designing a mechanism for the bomb itself, and, crucially, the horrendously difficult physical task of separating the rare uranium 235 isotope which had, hitherto, only been produced in sub-microscopic quantities. But advances taking place in California seemed to offer a possible escape from these difficulties.

Doctor Glenn Theodore Seaborg was a tall, thin gangling young man of Swedish American extraction. Although born in Michigan, he had grown up in California, living in Los Angeles and taking a chemistry PhD at Berkeley in 1937. Seaborg's great scientific interest was the chemistry of radioactive materials – radiochemistry – and he was a close follower of the work of Otto Hahn. In 1939 he had been excited to hear of the discovery of fission, but disappointed as well. On the day that the news broke at Berkeley, Seaborg had wandered the streets into the early hours of the morning, pondering the breakthrough:

> I was disgusted with myself that I had not seen this explanation. It seemed so beautifully obvious. I had had all the clues. Alvarez, Oppenheimer, Segré – we'd all had the same clues, and we had failed. Like Bohr, each of us was saying – how could we have missed this?

What was left for Seaborg and his collaborators was the search for elements beyond uranium in the periodic table; elements that did not exist in the natural state on earth but which might be produced in the laboratory, transmuted as the alchemists of the middle ages had hoped to do, but by bombardment with neutrons.

The first transuranic element, neptunium, was discovered

in the spring of 1940 at Berkeley by Edwin McMillan and Philip Abelson, who were conducting experiments to measure the 'range' of fragments of uranium elements after fission. They discovered that U238 atoms would absorb a neutron, creating a new, unstable radioactive isotope 'U239' with a radioactive half-life of 2.3 days. Investigation proved this to be an element chemically different from any other known substance. In other words, men had succeeded in creating element number 93, or, as they named it following the planetary sequence after Uranus, neptunium.

But it seemed to McMillan that uranium might be the father of another element beyond neptunium; that the 'decay product' of neptunium might actually be element 94. This element, McMillan predicted, should be fissile in a similar way to uranium. He set to work to separate his neptunium samples chemically to achieve greater purity.

McMillan's search for element 94 came to a halt when he was called away to take part in the American development of radar in November 1940, following the visit of Sir Henry Tizard. Thereafter, it was left to Glenn Seaborg to follow the trail.

One of Seaborg's most difficult tasks was obtaining enough uranium to isolate his new element:

> Our supplies were always small till then. We could always get half-pound bottles of uranium nitrate from the chemical firms, but few carried anything like kilogram lots. I often had to seek elsewhere for experimental supplies. I once wrote to a man I'd heard had some residues from the old Bohemia mine Marie Curie used; I also chased supplies from Canada.

But he was able to get sufficient uranium to create fractions of a millionth of a gram of pure neptunium. These minute amounts were sufficient. During the night of Sunday 23 February, Seaborg and his colleague, chemist Art Wahl, succeeded in isolating a substance from their neptunium sample that showed unexpected levels of alpha radiation:

> our alpha activity can be separated from all known elements [including neptunium] and thus it is now clear that our alpha activity is due to the new element with the atomic number 94.

Seaborg told Wahl:

> We've done it Art! We've nailed down a new element, for sure.

Having discovered that neptunium decayed into a further element, the next step for Seaborg was to find out if the new substance was, indeed, fissile. On 28 March, he recorded:

> Sample A (estimated to contain 0.25 micrograms of 94) was placed near the screen window of the ionization chamber embedded in paraffin near the beryllium target of the 37-inch cyclotron. The neutrons produced by the irradiation of the beryllium target with 8 MeV deuterons give a fission rate of 1 count per minute per microampere. When the ionization chamber is surrounded by a cadmium shield, the fission rate drops to essentially zero.

Which led Seaborg to conclude that:

> This gives strong indications that 94 undergoes fission with slow neutrons.

The importance of this discovery was potentially immense. Separation of the two isotopes of uranium involved very difficult physical processes to part the two forms of the same material; but retrieving element 94 could be done using comparatively simple chemical methods. Provided that sufficient irradiated uranium could be provided, element 94 should prove to be a far more abundant source of the fissile material needed for bomb making.

Although a name was not formally adopted for the new element until 1942, Seaborg had the discoverers' right to choose it. He decided to follow the example of Klaproth, discoverer of uranium, and McMillan, discoverer of neptunium, and name the new element after the next planet in the solar system, which had, incidentally, itself only been discovered in 1930. After trying 'plutium' and deciding that it was not sufficiently sonorous, Seaborg settled on plutonium.

Planning for the uranium bomb project had proceeded since President Roosevelt's guarded approval for the scheme was granted at the start of 1942, under the supervision of Vannevar Bush and his OSRD, but it was not until September 1942 that an individual was appointed with full responsibility for the detailed co-ordination of one of the most important scientific projects in history. With proper regard to the hoped – for outcome, it was decided that the atom bomb needed a military officer with a sufficiently forceful personality – and with sufficient back-up – to force the project through. Bush discussed his requirements with General Brehon Somervell, who was in command of the Army Services of Supply, and settled on a 46-year-old graduate of West Point, Colonel Leslie R. Groves.

In 1942, Groves was the deputy chief of construction for the whole US army and, having just completed the supervision of the construction of the Pentagon building in Washington DC, he was hoping for an appointment commanding troops overseas in Europe or the Pacific. Instead, to his intense annoyance, General Somervell informed him that he was facing a change of assignment:

> It was on September 17, 1942, at 10.30 a.m. that I got the news. I had agreed, by noon that day, to telephone my acceptance of a proposed assignment to duty overseas. I was then a colonel in the Army Engineers, with most of the headaches of directing ten billion dollars' worth of military construction in the country behind me – for good, I hoped. I wanted to get out of Washington, and quickly.
>
> [Somervell] . . . met me in a corridor of the new House of Representatives office building when I had finished testifying about a construction project before the Military Affairs Committee.
>
> 'About that duty overseas,' General Somervell said, 'you can tell them no.'
>
> 'Why?', I enquired.
>
> 'The Secretary of War has selected you for a very important assignment.'
>
> 'Where?'
>
> 'Washington.'
>
> 'I don't want to stay in Washington.'
>
> 'If you do the job right' [he] said carefully, 'it will win the war.'

Groves questioned Somervell more closely to find out exactly what was expected of him. He discovered that he was to be in charge of a project which he had seen mentioned on requests for construction priorities; he thought it to be small potatoes. 'Oh! That thing', he said, disconsolately.

Groves was a big man in every sense of the word. He accepted the disappointment of not going overseas and resolved to make the best of what he supposed to be a bad job; in any event, he was a career soldier and was accustomed to obeying orders. But for all that Groves was a 'simple army officer' given a tough assignment, he undoubtedly had a sense of destiny; although he was later to be described as 'a corner cutter, a dimesaver . . . tough, tireless and resilient . . . he got things done', it was also said that 'He has the most impressive ego since Napoleon' and that 'he not only behaves as if he can walk on water, but as if he actually invented the substance'. One subordinate was later to remark:

> [he was the] biggest sonofabitch I've ever met in my life, but also one of the most capable individuals. He had an ego second to none, he had tireless energy – he was a big man, a heavy man but he never seemed to tire. He had absolute confidence in his decisions and he was absolutely ruthless in how he approached a problem to get it done. But that was the beauty of working for him – that you never had to worry about the decisions being made or what it meant. In fact I've often thought that if I were to have to do my part all over again, I would select Groves as boss. I hated his guts and so did everybody else but we had our form of understanding.

In appointing Groves to command the bomb project, Vannevar Bush had undoubtedly selected a man to be reckoned with. Ironically, one of the first people to discover this was Bush himself. The first and 'master' principle of military operations is 'selection and maintenance of the aim'. Groves was to show that he had taken his military training to heart.

One of Bush's earliest attachments to the OSRD was another colonel of engineers, James C. Marshall, who had cloaked the atomic bomb project in the disguise of the

'Manhattan Engineer District'. When Groves took over the organization, one of his first priorities was to a pay a visit to the head of the OSRD, it did not turn out well. Groves had already discovered from his military subordinates that the uranium bomb project was founded on 'possibility rather than probability' and that the techniques and raw materials were uncertain at best. Groves had been given the rank of brigadier general (one star) on appointment to the post, but he was determined to outface the presidential appointee Bush. This he succeeded in doing; Bush reported that Groves was 'blunt' and that he 'doubted whether he had sufficient tact for the job'.

In fact Groves proved that tact had no part in it; a principal concern that faced the Manhattan Engineer District was a shortage of raw materials and particularly uranium. His subordinate Nichols told Groves that 1,250 tons of uranium ore was stored on a quayside on Staten Island, New York; Groves sent Nichols to buy it: problem solved. Groves' next move was to draft a letter over the signature of the head of the War Production Board assigning the Manhattan Engineer District 'AAA' priority in all supply matters; the board chairman demurred until Groves told him that the president of the United States would be most upset to hear of the project's cancellation because the war production board would not co-operate. Faced with these examples of Groves' ability, Bush quickly warmed to him.

Groves' purchase of the 1,250 tons of uranium ores made possible one of the most important experiments to be conducted before the bomb itself was built: a controlled nuclear chain reaction. In early 1942, Fermi, Szilard and their associates, who had been working together at Columbia University in New York, moved to the new 'Metallurgical Laboratory' (known as Met-Lab), which had been set up by Arthur Compton at the University of Chicago under the auspices of the OSRD. Fermi had begun planning a chain-reacting 'pile' in May, and by October, when the uranium began to arrive, work was well in hand. The original site for the pile was the Argonne Forest Reserve just over twenty miles from Chicago, but the construction workers who were being employed for the project decided to strike. Fermi examined his options and concluded that he could safely build a chain reactor in a disused 'doubles' squash court under the west stand of the Chicago University sports stadium, in the heart of Chicago's southern suburbs.

Work began on the first nuclear reactor on 16 November 1942. Fermi had ordered a 25-foot 'square' balloon from the Goodyear company within which to build the pile, so as to exclude air, and the bottom of this was smoothed onto the floor; a circle with a diameter of 19 feet was drawn onto it with a stick of chalk and construction started.

The pile was designed as a sphere of graphite blocks held up by a wooden framework. The graphite was drilled to accept small spheres of uranium oxide, which were inserted as the pile was built, and neutron activity was controlled by the use of long wooden rods with strips of cadmium attached. At the end of each shift, as the pile took shape, Walter Zinn and Herbert Anderson, another of Fermi's senior collaborators, measured the activity in the pile with the cadmium control rods removed. As each new layer was added, neutron activity increased towards the point where a chain reaction would begin.

Outside the squash court, winter was setting in. This produced two effects: firstly it was noted that lower temperatures seemed to increase neutron intensity; and secondly the security guards began to freeze! This problem was easily solved:

The University came to the rescue. Years before, big league

football had been banned from the campus: we found in an old locker a supply of raccoon fur coats. Thus, for a time we had the best dressed collegiate style guards in the business.

As the purity of the uranium being supplied improved, Fermi calculated that the pile would be ready to go critical between the 56th and 57th layers, when the whole structure would be 20 feet high and 25 feet in diameter. The final part of the structure was completed under the supervision of Herbert Anderson during the night of 1 Decmber 1942:

> When the 57th layer was completed, I called a halt to the work, in accordance with the agreement we had reached in the meeting with Fermi that afternoon. All the cadmium rods but one were removed and the neutron count taken following the standard procedure which had been followed on the previous days. It was clear from the count that once the only remaining cadmium rod was removed, the pile would go critical. I resisted great temptation to pull the final cadmium strip and be the first to make a pile chain react. However Fermi had foreseen this temptation and extracted a promise from me to make the measurements, record the result, insert all cadmium rods, and lock them in place.

On the morning of 2 December 1942, Chicago was covered by a deep layer of snow. Fermi and his team trudged to the squash court to inaugurate the age of atomic power controlled by man. The pile that they had built contained 350 tons of graphite, 50 tons of uranium oxide and 6 tons of pure metallic uranium; it had cost over $1,000,000, in the days before inflation, but it looked like a roughly shaped structure of greasy black blocks and bare, timber shoring planks. The only visibly moving parts of the pile were the control and safety rods, some of which projected from the sides, two of them hanging above the reactor; these were the two fail-safe devices designed to stop the reaction if all else failed. One of these, designed by Walter Zinn and christened ZIP, was automatically operated if neutron activity got above a pre-set level. The second was slightly more crude: it consisted of a cadmium rod hanging on a rope with a young physicist standing next to it holding an axe; in the last resort, the physicist was to cut the rope with his axe and let gravity take the cadmium into the pile to absorb the neutrons. The final safety measure was a group of three physicists with jugs of cadmium sulphate solution, which they stood by to douse the reactor with if the control rods did not work. This caused some anxiety in the squash court because an accidental spillage from the jugs could have contaminated the pile and rendered it useless; fortunately this did not happen.

The experiment began around mid-morning as, one by one, the control rods were carefully drawn out of the pile and the scientists, installed with their measuring equipment in the spectators' gallery of the squash court, monitored the neutron levels. A small crowd began to gather as the last rod was drawn out to about halfway, leaving the reaction well below critical: Szilard and Wigner, the two Hungarian 'conspirators' who, through their friend Einstein, had first brought the nuclear threat to the attention of the US government, stood watching a landmark in the process that they had initiated. At about 11.30 a.m., as the last control rod was being drawn out yet further, ZIP, the automatic safety rod, interrupted proceedings by crashing into action as the radioactivity in the pile exceeded its programmed level. After a few moments, Fermi decided that this represented a good point to break for lunch, and the control rods were returned to the pile.

The experiment resumed at 2.00 p.m. Fermi ordered that all but the last rod be removed from the pile and checked the neutron readings. So far, as each control rod was removed, the pile intensity would rise and then level off, causing the monitoring instruments to click audibly at a steady pace, indicating that no chain reaction was taking place. Fermi told Compton, director of the Met-Lab, who had appeared at his side:

'This is going to do it. Now it will become self-sustaining. The trace will climb and continue to climb; it will not level off.'

Herbert Anderson described the scene:

At first you could hear the sound of the neutron counter, clickety-clack, clickety-clack . . . after a while they began to merge into a roar; the counter couldn't follow anymore. That was the moment to switch to the chart recorder [which traced activity on a roll of paper]. But when the switch was made, everyone watched in the sudden silence the mounting deflection of the recorder's pen. It was an awesome silence. Everyone realised the significance of that switch; we were in the high intensity regime and the counters couldn't cope with the situation anymore . . . Suddenly Fermi raised his hand. 'The pile has gone critical,' he announced. No one present had any doubt about it.

At 3.53 p.m. Fermi ordered that the safety rod be returned to the pile and the chain reaction stopped. The pile had been critical for 4.5 minutes. It had conclusively demonstrated that the chain reaction was fact. Wigner produced a bottle of chianti and some paper cups as Compton shook Fermi's hand. After the senior scientists had quietly drunk their chianti, the group began to disperse as the experimental team shut the reactor down. Compton went off to telephone his boss, James Conant of the NDRC, using a phrase that has gone down in history. Security requirements forced them to use veiled speech:

'Jim,' I said, 'you'll be interested to know that the Italian navigator has just landed in the new world.' Then, half apologetically, because I had led the S-I Committee to believe that it would be another week or more before the pile could be completed, I added, 'the earth was not as large as he had estimated, and he arrived in the new world sooner than he had expected.'

'Is that so,' was Conant's excited response. 'Were the natives friendly?'

'Everyone landed safe and happy.'

Another of the witnesses met Glenn Seaborg, who had recently moved his research to the Met-Lab, in a corridor. Seaborg realized that the success of the pile meant that plutonium, whose secrets he was still teasing out, could now be produced on an industrial scale in full-size reactors based on natural uranium. But Seaborg was also worried:

We have no way of knowing if this is the first chain reaction achieved. The Germans may have beaten us! I wonder – are they aware that elements made in a chain reaction of uranium isotopes can be used in an atomic bomb? And, if they do have a pile that reacts, will they use it to generate power, or produce vast amounts of radioactivity as a military weapon . . .?

Szilard waited with Fermi, quietly looking over the reactor, until everyone else had dispersed. They shook hands and Szilard told Fermi that: '[he] thought this day would go down as a black day in the history of mankind.'

It had been recognized at an early stage of the United States' government's involvement in the bomb project that alongside the overall project leader, the role that was fulfilled by Groves, there was a requirement for a scientific director – a nuclear physicist with the necessary co-ordinating and leadership skills to weld the several apparently disparate scientific strands of the project into practical bomb making. The man who was selected was Dr J. Robert Oppenheimer.

Oppenheimer was born into a wealthy, non-practising Jewish family in Manhattan on 22 April 1904. They lived on Riverside Drive, overlooking the Hudson River, and kept a summer house on fashionable Long Island. Oppenheimer's father, Julius, had emigrated from Germany at the age of 17 in 1898 and made a fortune importing textiles when ready-made clothing was just taking off. One consequence of his family's comparative wealth was that Oppenheimer had a very protected, loving childhood with few of the traumas and anxieties that most families go through; he later remarked that his childhood: 'did not prepare [him] for the fact that the world is full of cruel and bitter things. It gave [him] no normal, healthy way to be a bastard.' By the time that he reached Harvard, in 1922, he was intensely naive but intellectually strikingly gifted.

As a student Oppenheimer showed himself to be extremely versatile. Although he was majoring in chemistry, he also took courses in mathematics, physics, philosophy and even French literature; at the same time he would attend lectures on other subjects that took his fancy. Physically also, he blossomed. As he had always been weak and sickly as a child, his father arranged for him to spend time in the summer before going to Harvard hiking and riding in the mountains of New Mexico. The experience toughened him considerably and enabled him to cope with his heavy, self-imposed workload without great difficulty. He graduated 'summa cum laude' after three years.

After Harvard, Oppenheimer was determined to get to the 'centre' of science and managed to gain acceptance by Rutherford's Cavendish laboratory in Cambridge. But there he began to run into problems. Although trained as a chemist, Oppenheimer was a weak experimentalist, being happier in the world of theoretical exploration and analysis. He did not adapt well to the conditions at the Cavendish and he found the social *froideur* of the largely British staff uncomfortable. Always introspective, Oppenheimer began to suffer from profound depressions and thoughts of suicide. His parents sent him to a London psychiatrist, who misdiagnosed schizophrenia; despite this he managed to recover his equilibrium, although he remained touched by a deep melancholia throughout his life. As his psychiatric well-being improved, Oppenheimer turned away from experimental science and towards theoretical physics, the discipline that became his vocation, and it was in the field of quantum theory that he made his mark. In the period 1926–29, when Oppenheimer was working at Cambridge and at the University of Gottingen in Germany, he managed to publish sixteen scientific papers and establish himself as a theoretical physicist of the top rank. He returned to America to receive job offers from Harvard, the California Institute of Technology (Caltech) and Berkeley. Ever keen to stretch himself, he arranged to take both the Berkeley and Caltech jobs.

Probably the most controversial aspect of Oppenheimer's life and career resulted from the views that he developed and the political causes that he supported during the

1930s in California. He was introduced to Marxism by a Communist girlfriend, Jean Tatlock, with whom he came close to marriage. Although he never accepted or really understood Marx's writings, he came to identify with the cause of the Republicans in the Spanish Civil War, who were then fighting with the support of the Soviet Union against Franco's German- and Italian-supported Fascists; and, as a Jew, he was naturally outraged by Nazi persecution in Germany. Through Jean he associated with many people who were Communists of one sort or another and in fact met the woman that he did eventually marry. Oppenheimer's wife Kitty was also problematic; she had been married to an American Communist official who was killed in Spain, Joe Dallet, and had been a member of the Party for two years before she left in a state of disillusion.

Eventually Oppenheimer abandoned left-wing causes as his political views matured and his leadership skills, as Berkeley's senior theoretical physicist, increased. Pearl Harbor finally convinced him that there were causes in the world far more important than the leftist fads of his old associates, and he threw himself wholeheartedly into the bomb project. Oppenheimer first met Groves in October 1942, but he was already certain that some aspects of the scientific work on the bomb were not as efficient as they could be:

> I became convinced, as did others, that a major change was called for in the work on the bomb itself. We needed a central laboratory devoted wholly to this purpose, where people could talk freely with each other, where theoretical ideas and experiment findings could affect each other, where the waste and frustration and error of the many compartmentalised experimental studies could be eliminated, where we could

begin to come to grips with chemical, metallurgical, engineering and ordnance problems that had so far received no
consideration.

Groves thought about security in military terms – that
it was best that as few people as possible should have
access to the whole picture – but Oppenheimer's advocacy
convinced him. He accepted that Oppenheimer was right
and decided that he should direct the laboratory himself.
It was then that Oppenheimer's Communist connections
began to interfere, as US army counter-intelligence refused
to sanction his appointment. Groves fought his corner hard
– with the power delegated to him by the president, he was
unwilling to take no for an answer – and he succeeded in
persuading the Military Policy Committee that there was no
alternative to Oppenheimer, although he conceded that the
scientist, who had committed no illegal act, would have to
remain under surveillance. (When Groves later tried to stop
this surveillance, his subordinates ignored his orders.)

With Oppenheimer installed as director of the notional
laboratory, the next step was actually to find a location for
it. Groves specified that 'Site Y', as it was known, would
need to have room for 265 people, be at least 200 miles
from any international border, and west of the Mississippi.
Oppenheimer, for his part, was keen to select a site near to
the area of New Mexico he had explored as a teenager, in
the summer before he went to Harvard, and where he now
maintained a run-down farmhouse with his brother Frank.
In the end Groves and Oppenheimer settled on the site of a
remote boys' school about twenty miles outside Santa Fé in
the foothills of the Rocky Mountains: Los Alamos Ranch.

So the autumn and winter of 1942–3 saw the commence-
ment of work on the Los Alamos laboratory, where the
practical problems of constructing atomic weapons were

to be resolved, and it also saw Oppenheimer begin the recruitment of those scientists who were actually to do it. In England, the process was reasonably easy, as Otto Frisch describes:

> one day Chadwick came to me and in his usual direct manner asked 'How would you like to work in America?' I said 'I would like that very much'. 'But then you would have to become a British citizen.' 'I would like that even more', I said.

Such was the importance of the project that the normal British passion for dithering and bureaucracy was entirely circumvented in the case of a small group of scientists who were, technically at least, enemy aliens. Frisch again:

> Within a few days a policeman appeared and started to take down personal data as well as the names of people who knew me and could vouch for me, explaining that he had been instructed to start naturalisation proceedings. He added in an oddly confiding manner, 'You must be a pretty big shot; I have been told to get everything done within a week!' And indeed it was only about a week later that I got instructions to pack all my necessary belongings into one suitcase and to come to London by the night train, to a government office in Old Queen Street.
>
> There a tall lady secretary acted like a maitre de ballet, sending off each scientist on a new errand as soon as he came back from the last one. I was sent to a magistrate, who took my Oath of Allegiance to His Majesty the King; in return he gave me a document which stated that I was now a British citizen. Back at the office I was told to go and obtain release from military service, otherwise I was a deserter! Then I was sent to pick up a passport, ready

for me, and with that I went to the American Embassy where somebody was waiting to stamp my visa into the new passport.

However, the process was slightly complicated in the United States by General Groves' initial intention that the US scientists would be commissioned into the US army as officers and that the laboratory would be a military post commanded by 'Lieutenant-Colonel' Oppenheimer. Neither Groves nor Oppenheimer expected the strong resistance that they discovered to this idea. They eventually compromised on the scientific personnel remaining civilians until large-scale trials had commenced; in the end, this was not enforced.

By the time that research started in earnest at Los Alamos in April 1943, the scientists involved in the project were happy that, theoretically at least, uranium 235 and plutonium 239 could, in certain circumstances, be induced into an explosive chain reaction in manageably small quantities. Further, several of them, including Enrico Fermi and particularly the Hungarian Edward Teller, had conjectured that, by using an atomic explosion as an initiator, it might be possible to cause a 'fusion' reaction in atoms of 'heavy' hydrogen, mimicking the reactions that take place in the stars and creating vastly more powerful weapons. The task that Groves and Oppenheimer devised for them, and which was discussed at a conference in April 1943, was to produce a *practical* military weapon which could be used when sufficient quantities of separated U235 and Pu239 became available.

As the Los Alamos laboratory was being constructed and its staff recruited, work also began on the gigantic production plants necessary to separate out the raw materials for the bombs. After some debate it had been agreed that equal priority would be given to developing both electromagnetic and gaseous diffusion techniques to separate U235 from natural uranium. Electromagnetic separation depended on the fact that electrically charged atoms of uranium would, when passed through a vacuum influenced by a strong magnetic field, separate out into 'beams' of the two different atomic weights and could thus, in theory, be collected. The chief proponent of the system, Ernest O. Lawrence of Berkeley, calculated that 2,000 individual separation units would be needed to produce 100 grams of U235 per day. Groves accepted this but argued that, by the time the units were built, the technique would have been improved and higher production rates would be achieved; he ordered 500 units and work began on building the plant, at Oak Ridge in Tennessee, in February 1943. The gaseous diffusion plant was also built at Oak Ridge. This method involved passing uranium hexafluoride gas through a 'cascade' of thousands of porous barriers, after each of which the 'enriched' gas would tend to rise into the next stage whilst the depleted gas would go down for collection and recycling. Despite considerable early difficulties, both systems were on stream by early 1944, producing sufficient U235, it was estimated, to build a functioning bomb – or 'gadget', as it became known in the Los Alamos jargon – in the first few months of 1945.

Plutonium production was not to be carried out at Oak Ridge. Although the risks were deemed to be small, it was decided that Oak Ridge was too close to Knoxville for comfort. Instead, Groves selected the tiny riverside village of Hanford in Washington State as the site for the plutonium production reactors. Work began in the late summer of 1943 and the first of the piles was assembled in February 1944. The design, which was by Eugene Wigner, required slugs of uranium to be irradiated in the pile for 100 days – sufficient to transmute one atom in 4,000 into plutonium

– and then cooled for a further 60 days, before being taken to the chemical separation plants, shielded behind hills a few miles away.

With the Oak Ridge and Hanford plants manufacturing the raw materials for the bombs, Los Alamos was now fully committed to weapon design. In essence the task was to produce a mechanism that would assemble a critical mass of U235 or Pu239 in the shortest possible time. The easiest way to do this seemed to be to make a gun that would fire a bullet of U235 into a target of the same material, thus making, in a split second, a single lump of sufficient size to undergo a chain reaction.

But there seemed to be two problems with this approach. In the first place, the scientists needed to be sure that the two pieces of uranium met sufficiently quickly for there to be ample material present for a full divergent chain reaction of at least eighty generations, but that it did not start too early. Secondly, it was essential that there were sufficient neutrons present so that the chain reaction started before the 'target' U235 broke under the impact of the bullet. In both of these scenarios, premature and late detonation, it was anticipated that the assembly would 'fizzle' with the explosive power of a 'mere' 60 or so tons of TNT. The two solutions that they decided to pursue actively at this stage were the use of an extremely high-velocity gun to fire the fissile materials together, and the placing of a polonium/beryllium neutron source in the uranium as an initiator; but another option was suggested and began to be explored. This was that it might be feasible to 'implode' a sphere of fissile material by wrapping it in explosives, thus achieving a virtually instantaneous critical mass.

Despite the grimness of their task, an extraordinary atmosphere prevailed at Los Alamos. Otto Frisch recalled that:

Oppie had recruited not only the chemists, physicists and engineers that the project required but also a painter, a philosopher and a few other unlikely characters; he felt that a civilised community would be incomplete without them. The scientists that had come included some of the very cream of American universities, and I had the pleasant notion that if I struck out in an arbitrary direction and knocked on the first door that I saw I would find interesting people inside, engaged in making music or in stimulating conversation. I have certainly never seen a town with such a variety of intelligent and cultured people.

One such was the young theoretical physicist Richard Feynman, whom, according to Frisch, 'everyone recognised as a budding genius':

He worked out how a combination lock functioned and after that he could open other peoples' safes by just listening to the tiny clicks that could be heard when the knob was turned forward and backward in the prescribed manner; he embarrassed some people either by leaving their safes open so that they were scolded by the security officer, or by leaving mysterious messages inside.

The long process of refining the technical specifications of the bomb continued in parallel with the production of fissile material throughout 1943 and 1944. But whilst the raw materials of bomb production were essential to the project, so was a delivery system. Early calculations of the size of the bomb concluded that, including the extremely dense uranium, the trigger mechanism and the casing, it was likely to weigh several tons and be of considerable length and bulk. The only Allied aircraft then capable of carrying such a weapon without major modification was the British Lancaster, the RAF's principle heavy bomber. But to use a British aircraft to drop what had become, to all intents and purposes, an American weapon was unacceptable to the US army, who now had effective control of the project. Instead they looked towards a plane that was then in the early stages of production, the new B-29 Superfortress.

The Superfortress was, in 1944, still a controversial aircraft. In February 1943 one of the early prototypes had crashed into a factory in Seattle, killing the crew and a number of workers, and some air force personnel held it to be unflyable. Despite this, it had been specifically designed as a heavy-load, high-altitude, long-range bomber. The crew compartments were pressurized, enabling it to cruise for long distances above 30,000 feet, well out of range of most anti-aircraft weaponry and the majority of contemporary fighter aircraft; and it was capable of carrying a bomb load of 20,000 lbs. The only serious disadvantage for the atomic bomb project was that the B-29's bomb bay was divided into two sections, both too short for the projected length of the 'gun-type' weapon; but this could be remedied without overwhelming difficulty. In all other respects, it was ideal.

But in addition to the 'perfect' aircraft, Groves and the Military Policy Committee felt that they needed perfect crews to man them and drop the bombs. The stakes in the Manhattan Project were simply too high to allow the possibility that the bombs might be dropped in the wrong place or 'handed over' to the enemy through some grotesque human error. Eighteen B-29s were being specially modified during the summer of 1944, but the man who was selected to command them, train the crews and, ultimately, fly the mission to bomb Hiroshima did not learn of his appointment until 1 September 1944.

Lieutenant-Colonel Paul W. Tibbets was then 29 years

of age. He had been training to be a doctor but, in 1936, gave up his medical studies to learn to fly with the US army air corps. By 1944 he was probably one of the most experienced and skilled bomber pilots in the US air force; he had flown 43 combat missions over Europe and, perhaps just as importantly, had been deeply involved in the flight testing of the B-29. Alongside his flying skills and military abilities, Tibbets was also a cultured and sensitive man with the ability to lead and to command respect from his subordinates. When, on 1 September, he was summoned to the office of Major-General Uzal Ent, commanding the 2nd Air Force at Colorado Springs, to learn of his new appointment, he faced a subtle and embarrassing test. Colonel John Lansdale, Groves' security chief for the Manhattan Project, intercepted Tibbets in General Ent's ante-room and asked him directly: had Tibbets ever been arrested?

Lansdale knew the answer and knew that it would require Tibbets to swallow his pride before telling an unknown officer of equal rank, but Tibbets' habitual honesty stood him in good stead. Yes, Tibbets admitted, the police chief at North Miami Beach had arrested him as a teenager in the back of a car with a girl. Lansdale, who had spent the previous 48 hours conducting an extensive vetting of Tibbets' background, announced himself satisfied, and Ent, assisted by Captain 'Deke' Parsons and Norman Ramsey of Los Alamos, briefed Tibbets on the extraordinary task that faced him.

Tibbets learned that he would be responsible for con-verting the 393rd Bombardment Squadron from a standard air force outfit into an elite team capable of successfully initiating the age of atomic warfare. He was given a training base, at Wendover Field, Utah, and his pick of the best aircrew in the US air force. The code name for the US air force involvement was 'Silverplate', and its use would guarantee Tibbets the highest priority in everything he needed. The downside of his job was also spelled out to the young colonel – he had to be prepared to work alongside:

> a bunch of civilians who would give [him] a glimpse inside Pandora's box.

General Ent also told him:

> Colonel, if this is successful, you'll be a hero. But if it fails, you'll be the biggest scapegoat ever. You may even go to prison.

A week later, Tibbets flew down to Wendover.

By the time that Tibbets began his task of moulding an air force unit capable of dropping atomic weapons, it was becoming increasingly clear that the war in Europe – against Nazi Germany – was going to be all but over before the bombs were ready for testing, let alone operational use. The fear of German nuclear weapons had been the original impetus driving the Manhattan Project towards its final goal, but this now appeared to be receding. Allied intelligence had become aware of the German nuclear physicists' reliance on heavy water in their experimentation, and had mounted a sustained campaign against the Germans' only source, the Norsk Hydro plant at Rjukan in occupied Norway. This had included a commando attack by British-trained Norwegians in February 1943 that had put back production by two years; a precision bombing raid by the US air force in November 1943 that had effectively shut production down; and finally a second sabotage mission that had sent the surviving stocks of heavy water to the bottom of a deep fjord in February 1944. In any event, the senior German physicists, whose spokesman was Heisenberg, had largely reached the conclusion that an atomic bomb project would require too many resources in Germany in wartime and would, therefore, not be feasible; a conclusion that they passed to Hitler's armaments minister, Albert Speer, in the autumn of 1942. Thereafter their research, which continued at a low level, was largely aimed at building a nuclear reactor for the generation of power.

The fact that the Germans had essentially given up in their attempts to build an atomic bomb did not percolate through to Allied intelligence until the war's end, but, with the situation becoming more and more favourable for Allied operations in 1944, a scheme was launched to try and collect as much information as possible on the German efforts by sending Manhattan Project personnel into the field to attempt to round up the key nuclear scientists in occupied Europe as they were overrun. At the same time Heisenberg, perceived as the most dangerous of the German physicists, became the subject of several kidnap and assassination plans.

The mission to uncover the secrets of German nuclear research was code named ALSOS and commanded by Lieutenant-Colonel Boris T. Pash of US army G-2 Security. Having established a base in London, he led teams of soldiers and scientists that moved with the foremost elements of the Allied armies, seizing documents and interviewing scientists of the occupied countries as they went, building the evidence that Germany had got nowhere with its bomb project. Documents captured by ALSOS as the Allies swept across the Rhine into Germany at the beginning of 1945 indicated that the senior German physicists were mostly working in southern Germany, away from the heaviest bombing. On 17 April 1945, an ALSOS team commanded

by Colonel John Lansdale discovered the German stockpile
of uranium ore in an open-sided shed at a factory in Stassfurt
near Magdeburg; on 23 April, Pash, Lansdale and a few
of their colleagues forced the lock on a doorway leading
into a cave in the village of Haigerloch. There they found
a cylindrical pit lined with graphite and covered by a
heavy metal lid: the remains of the last German reactor.
Michael Perrin, a British officer with the group, quickly
realized that it could never have gone critical – there was
no shielding and the radiation would have killed everyone
in the cave. By now, most of the senior German scientists
were 'guests' in the custody of ALSOS; the intention was
to isolate them in England and debrief them on German
research. With Heisenberg picked up on 3 May, ALSOS had
obtained a crop of some of the most respected international
scientists: Otto Hahn, Max von Laue, Carl-Friedrich von
Weiszacker and of course Heisenberg himself were men
with world reputations; Diebner, Bagge, Gerlach, Harteck
and Korsching, the others who were detained, had all been
significant players in nuclear physics under the Third Reich.
None of them believed that the Allies could be much further
advanced than they were in atomic research. They were
flown out of Europe, to a country house near Cambridge,
on 3 July 1945.

Research at Los Alamos in the summer of 1944 had
revealed a potentially catastrophic problem with plutonium
as a bomb material: the spontaneous fission rate was too
high and in a gun-type bomb it was probable that a
premature detonation would cause it to 'fizzle' and melt
down without achieving a satisfactory explosion. The only
way that it seemed possible that plutonium would work –
and for various reasons plutonium appeared to be a more
suitable material than uranium – was in an implosion bomb.
In consequence, a great deal of effort was then expended

on discovering how to start a detonation wave that would travel spherically into a sphere. The technology that seemed most likely to offer a solution was to be found in 'shaped charges' and 'explosive lenses'. Earlier in the war it had been noted that, by varying the shape of the surface of an explosive charge, it appeared possible to 'focus' the detonation wave in such a way as to achieve far greater effects than would have been possible with an unshaped charge. As Los Alamos waited for U235 for the comparatively simple gun-type bomb, the new X-division there sought to find a combination of shape and explosive that would implode a plutonium sphere.

A review of progress by Groves and his civilian superior James Conant at the end of 1944 was optimistic about the prospects for the project: Groves expected to begin serial production of plutonium and uranium bombs in the second half of 1945. Conant noted that:

> It looks like a race to see whether a [plutonium bomb] or a [uranium bomb] will be dropped first and whether the month will be July, August or September.

But at that stage, nobody was really sure how much TNT equivalent the bombs would yield or even if the plutonium bomb would explode: the implosion method could not be assessed without a full-scale test. On the other hand, a series of experiments conducted by Frisch at Los Alamos had proved the readiness of U235 to chain react explosively.

Frisch's experiments were reasonably simple: they involved creating an untamped critical mass for a brief moment and measuring the radioactivity that this produced:

> The idea was that the . . . U235 should indeed be assembled to make [an explosive device] . . . but leaving a big hole

so that the central portion was missing; that would allow enough neutrons to escape so that no chain reaction could develop. But the missing portion was to be made, ready to be dropped through that hole so that for a split second there was the condition for an atomic explosion, although only barely so.

. . . It was as near as we could possibly go towards starting an atomic explosion without actually being blown up, and the results were most satisfactory. Everything happened exactly as it should. When the core was dropped through the hole we got a large burst of neutrons and a temperature rise of several degrees in that very short split second during which the chain reaction proceeded as a sort of stifled explosion.

Richard Feynman nicknamed this series of tests the 'Dragon Experiments', because they were 'like tickling the tail of a sleeping dragon'. They proved, as far as it could be proved, that the gun-type uranium bomb would work.

To test the plutonium implosion bomb required a critical mass of the metal itself and a large, empty area to do it in. This was found in an area of scrub and desert 210 miles south of Los Alamos on the northern edge of the Alamogordo bombing range, which had been known, since Spanish times, as the Jornada del Muerto or 'journey of death'. For the purposes of the experiment, the site was codenamed 'Trinity'.

Rather than dropping a bomb from an aircraft, it was decided that the best way to set off the world's first atomic explosion would be from a tall steel tower mounted firmly on the ground. Construction began on the 100-foot-high tower towards the end of April; simultaneously work started to install the myriad monitoring devices that would automatically record the test.

Timing for the explosion was dictated by the availability of the plutonium and the explosive 'lenses' that would implode it. The metal was prepared at Los Alamos and was ready by 24 June, but the explosives were taking longer. By 9 July there were still insufficent high-quality castings of explosive to make both the bomb and a full-scale, 'non-atomic' copy that Oppenheimer had ordered tested a few days before the real event. As preparations continued, a tentative date was set for the experiment: 16 July.

The tension for those closely involved in the test was great. George Kistiakowsky, who was responsible for the design and assembly of the implosion charge, had found by X-raying his explosives that they were riddled with small holes that would disturb the spherical wave. He sat up for a night hand-drilling through to them and filling them with molten explosive, reasoning that if the 50-lb blocks went off, he would know nothing about it. But more worrying news followed; when the replica charge was detonated at Los Alamos, measurements indicated that it would not have set off an implosion bomb. Groves, Oppenheimer, Bush and Conant took it in turns to excoriate Kistiakowsky for his incompetence. According to Kistiakowsky:

> At another point Oppenheimer became so emotional that I offered him a month's salary against ten dollars that our implosion charge would work.

Oppenheimer accepted this bet but was, nevertheless, relieved when later the same day Hans Bethe, at Los Alamos, proved that the instrumentation used was bound to cause the depressing reading that was obtained in the replica test.

Two days before the test, the first experimental atomic bomb was hauled to the top of the steel tower at the bottom of which were standing, amongst others, Otto Frisch and Kistiakowsky. Frisch asked:

'How far away would we have to be for safety in case it went off?'

'Oh', he said, 'probably ten miles.'

'So in that case we might as well stay and watch the fun.'

Eventually it was agreed that the bomb would be detonated at dawn on 16 July. As the hour of the test approached, the various spectators dealt with their anxieties in their own ways. Enrico Fermi, who only two years before had calmly handled the first *controlled* chain reaction in the Chicago squash court, irritated General Groves and frightened some of the soldiers guarding the site when he:

offered to take wagers from his fellow scientists on whether or not the bomb would ignite the atmosphere, and if so, whether it would merely destroy New Mexico or destroy the world.

Some others succeeded in sleeping, some in reading. Otto Frisch dozed in a car, vaguely listening to dance music being played over the loudspeakers; Emilio Segré watched hundreds of frogs mating in a pool of water left by the thunderstorms that occasionally drenched the area. Groves and Oppenheimer harried and occasionally harangued the weather forecaster, pressuring him to give them a time when the weather would be clear enough for the test. At the bomb site, 'point zero', Kenneth Bainbridge, who was in charge of the test, was concerned that lightning might strike the bomb on its steel tower and set it off. At 4.40 a.m. the weather forecaster called Bainbridge and they decided to go ahead at 5.30. Bainbridge informed Oppenheimer and Groves, threw the arming switch and left for the firing point 10,000 yards (about six miles) away from the bomb.

The earth-and-concrete bunker at the firing point was crowded. Together with the personnel actually setting off the bomb were Oppenheimer, Groves' deputy Farrell and several others; Groves himself went by mutual agreement to the base camp in order to be physically separated from Farrell if anything went disastrously wrong. The timing sequence was started 20 minutes before the bomb was due to be detonated, and a flare was fired from the bunker to signal this. The majority of the spectators were about twenty miles from point zero, but even there precautions were in order; most of them were using thick welders' glass to protect their eyes from the anticipated bright flash, and Edward Teller solemnly passed sun oil around a group of observers that included Ernest Lawrence, Hans Bethe and James Chadwick. At 5.29 the one-minute warning rocket was fired into the air; Kistiakowsky, who expected a 1-kiloton yield (equivalent to 1,000 tons of TNT) left the firing-point bunker to stand outside in what he assumed would be safety. Frisch, fourteen miles further back:

> sat on the ground in case the explosion blew me over, plugged my ears with my fingers, and looked in the direction away from the explosion as I listened to the end of the count.

At 5.29 and 45 seconds the automatic firing circuit snapped closed and a specially designed unit simultaneously fired 32 detonators into the explosive casing of the bomb. The detonation wave formed a sphere, driving inward, and in a brief fraction of a second the heavy uranium tamper and the plutonium core imploded, almost instantaneously creating a super-critical mass. The polonium/beryllium initiator showered neutrons into the plutonium ball and the chain reaction started. Twenty miles away, Otto Frisch was sitting with his back to the action:

... five, four, three, two, one ...

And then, without a sound, the sun was shining; or so it looked. The sand hills at the edge of the desert were shimmering in a very bright light, almost colourless and shapeless. This light did not seem to change for a couple of seconds and then began to dim. I turned round, but that object on the horizon which looked like a small sun was still too bright to look at. I kept blinking and trying to take looks, and after another ten seconds or so it had grown and dimmed into something more like a huge oil fire, with a structure that made it look a bit like a strawberry. It was slowly rising into the sky from the ground, with which it remained connected by a lengthening grey stem of swirling dust; incongruously, I thought of a red-hot elephant standing balanced on its trunk. Then, as the cloud of hot gas cooled and became less red, one could see a blue glow surrounding it ...

In the wake of the flash came the blast wave. Kistiakowsky, watching from six miles away, was knocked off his feet, twenty miles away, Enrico Fermi had prepared a small experiment:

I tried to estimate its strength by dropping from about six feet small pieces of paper before, during and after the passage of the blast wave. Since, at the time, there was no wind, I could observe very distinctly and actually measure the displacement of the pieces of paper that were in the process of falling while the blast was passing. The shift was about 2.5 meters, which, at the time, I estimated to correspond to the blast that would be produced by ten thousand tons of TNT.

Frank Oppenheimer, watching with his elder brother, was amazed by the noise:

> It bounced on the rocks, and then it went – I don't know where else it bounced. But it never seemed to stop. Not like an ordinary echo with thunder. It just kept echoing back and forth in that Jornada del Muerto. It was a very scary time when it went off.
>
> And I just wish I could remember what my brother said, but I can't – but I think we just said, 'It worked.' I think that's what we said, both of us. 'It worked.'

At the base camp, a terrified army officer shouted: 'The longhairs have let it get away from them!', but amongst most of the onlookers, the mood was one of deep thought. The physicist and consultant to the project I. I. Rabi watched Oppenheimer return to the base camp:

> his walk was like 'High Noon' – I think it's the best I could describe it – this kind of strut. He'd done it.

Oppenheimer himself thought of a line from the *Bhagavad gita*, an ancient Hindu text:

> Now I am become death, the destroyer of worlds.

Bainbridge, who had organized the test, told Oppenheimer:

> Now we're all sons of bitches.

A sphere of plutonium about the size of a softball had

exploded with the force of 18,600 tons of TNT, it had turned the desert floor around point zero into glass and totally vapourized a 100-foot-high steel tower. The intention now was to explode similar devices over cities.

4

Little Boy and Fat Man

The first US air raid against Japan took place in April 1942. A small force of B-25 medium bombers under the command of General James Doolittle took off from the aircraft carrier USS *Hornet* and bombed Tokyo and three other Japanese cities. Without the fuel to return to the carrier, on which, in any case, they would not have been able to land, the bombers flew on to China where they were abandoned. Outraged by this 'violation' of their homeland, Japanese military authorities ordered the execution of three captured crew members, and several more were sentenced to life imprisonment. But it was to be more than two and a half years before the US air force returned to the skies above Japan. On 24 November 1944, a force of one hundred B-29s was launched against industrial targets north of Tokyo from Saipan in the Mariana Islands.

The first three months of the conventional bombing campaign against Japan were characterized by difficulties that the US air force had problems overcoming. The art of strategic bombing had been learned in Europe where, against the sophisticated German air defence system, it was discovered that to give crews and airframes the best chance of survival it was necessary to bomb from as high an altitude as possible, making it difficult for enemy fighter aircraft to operate and making the smallest possible target for anti-aircraft fire. The B-29 was designed with precisely these tactics in mind: theoretically it was capable of bombing from 35,000 feet – above the realistic operating ceiling of most contemporary fighters and out of range of all but the heaviest flak guns. But it was in attempting to do this that the problems lay. In the first place, the straightforward task of climbing to this great height with a full load of bombs and fuel placed an enormous strain on the engines, which had a tendency to overheat and catch fire; secondly, high-altitude winds – the jetstream – with a velocity of up to 150 miles per hour made aiming almost impossible; and finally, Japanese weather conditions were such that crews could only expect to have about six or seven clear bombing days per month on average.

The situation changed when General Curtis LeMay assumed command of 21st Bomber Command on 20 January 1945. LeMay was a self-made man who had worked his way up through the Ohio National Guard to become one of the US air force's leading air bombardment strategists. During February 1945 he analysed the difficulties that his B-29s were encountering and studied the targets that they were attempting to destroy. As this process continued, the war in Europe was approaching its end. LeMay's target analysis indicated that Japanese towns and cities were particularly vulnerable to incendiary attack because of the prevalence of wood as a construction material; he also noted that they were unprotected by light anti-aircraft artillery and that intelligence claimed that Japan had not developed a night-fighter aircraft. To these insights was added a further factor: on the night of 13 February 1945, 1,400 British aircraft attacked the south-east German city of Dresden with incendiary bombs, initiating a firestorm that killed perhaps 50,000 people. Eric Pleasants, a British traitor who was serving in the *Waffen-SS* and was then based in Dresden, watched the scene from some nearby hills:

> We heard the rumbling noise of the planes and the sound of the explosions and we went out to see what was happening – me, my wife and her parents – and we could see this bright orange glow from the city and flashes from bombs, I suppose, or other things exploding; we could smell the smoke from twenty miles away and after a while I noticed that there was a steady rain of cinders falling on us, carried all the way over by the wind.

When, the next day, he returned to his barracks through the devastated town, he felt ashamed of the destruction wrought by his countrymen.

LeMay's findings led him to conclude that the most effective way to attack the Japanese homeland would be to burn it by launching attacks at night from B-29s carrying incendiaries at low level. In this way the aircraft would fly too quickly over the target to be engaged by heavy anti-aircraft guns, would not be attacked by fighters, and would drop their bombs in a relatively tight pattern, optimizing conditions to create a firestorm. In the early hours of 10 March, 334 B-29s dropped over 2,000 tons of incendiaries on mainly residential districts of Tokyo. The effect was devastating: with the fires fanned by high winds, over 100,000 people were killed in a six-hour period.

LeMay's attack on Tokyo set the course for the continued conventional bombing of Japan in the spring and summer of 1945. Using the method pioneered over Tokyo with such outstanding success, it was possible for the air force commanders to imagine, as had the British bomber commander, Arthur Harris, that it might be possible to bomb Japan into submission without an invasion. Estimates of the likely casualty figures for invading Japan varied but few believed it could be less than 500,000, the vast majority of whom would be United States soldiers. After Tokyo, LeMay's B-29 fleet began a relentless bombardment of the major Japanese towns and cities with the intention of destroying civilian morale and war production facilities.

But as LeMay used his bombers for the step-by-step disruption of normal life in Japan, the first meeting was taking place, in the Pentagon building in Washington DC, of the committee which would select which Japanese cities were to be the targets for atomic bombing. The guidelines set out for the committee, which was chaired by Farrell, Groves' deputy, were straightforward: the members, who consisted of a mixture of military and scientific personnel, were to select a target that was less than 1,500 miles from the launch base, could be bombed visually and consisted of industrial and/or urban concentrations. Additionally Groves specified that:

the targets chosen should be places the bombing of which would most adversely affect the will of the Japanese people to continue the war. Beyond that, they should be military in nature . . . the targets should not have been previously damaged by air raids . . .

LeMay's campaign left little choice for the committee, which concluded:

Hiroshima is the largest untouched target not on the 21st Bomber Command priority list.

A second committee, known as the 'Interim Committee', was also formed, by Secretary of War Henry Stimson, with a similar though non-technical remit to oversee the use of the bombs. Following the death of President Franklin Roosevelt on 12 April 1945, his place had been taken by his vice-president, the long-serving Missouri senator Harry S. Truman, who had had no knowledge of the development of the atomic bomb or its supposed capabilities. Truman had decided, whilst the war lasted, to keep many of Roosevelt's cabinet appointees in place, but he was represented on the Interim Committee by James F. Byrnes, a close associate of Roosevelt's who was destined to be Truman's secretary of state. Although the ultimate decision on whether to use the bomb would depend on Truman, Byrnes knew far more about the project and had, at that time, a better feel for the issues involved. It was Byrnes who would advise Truman to go ahead and use the bomb.

But as the committees pondered how best to use the bomb, if it was to be used at all, others who had been involved in its development looked at the same issues. At the Chicago Met-Lab, scientists held a vote on what to do with the new weapons:

1. Use them in the manner that is from the military point of view the most effective in bringing about prompt Japanese surrender at minimum human cost to our Armed Forces (23 votes).
2. Give a military demonstration in Japan to be followed by renewed opportunity for surrender before full use of the weapon is employed (69 votes).
3. Give an experimental demonstration in this country, with representatives of Japan present; followed by a new opportunity to surrender before full use of the weapon is employed (39 votes).

4. Withhold military use of the weapons, but make public experimental demonstration of their effectiveness (16 votes).

5. Maintain as secret as possible all developments of our new weapons and refrain from using them in this war (3 votes).

The Met-Lab vote was, of course, ignored; nevertheless, there was a considerable debate at a high level about whether there should be some form of demonstrative action before the bomb was used operationally, to give the Japanese government a chance to consider their position. The Interim Committee gave some thought to the idea but eventually concluded:

> that we could not give the Japanese any warning; that we could not concentrate on a civilian area; but that we should seek to make a profound psychological impression on as many of the inhabitants as possible . . . the most desirable target would be a vital war plant employing a large number of workers and closely surrounded by workers' houses.

The last meeting of the target committee took place on 28 May, when it was decided that three targets would be preserved from bombing by LeMay's 21st Bomber Command: Kyoto, Japan's former capital, Hiroshima and Niigata; and that the decision as to which would ultimately be bombed would be made in accordance with weather and other conditions on the day of the operation. It was necessary to stop bombing these cities so that damage caused by the atomic bombs could be assessed; such was LeMay's programme that he expected to have bombed every strategic target flat by the beginning of 1946.

Thus it was that the decision, in principle, to use the bombs as well as the selection of likely targets had taken place some time before the first experimental explosion at Trinity. But on 14 July, even as the Trinity test was being prepared, the 'working parts' of the U235 gun-type bomb were being shipped out of Los Alamos on the first leg of their journey to the Pacific, under heavy escort.

A few hours after the prototype plutonium bomb had lit up the New Mexico dawn, the gun assembly and projectile of its uranium cousin arrived at a dockside in San Francisco ready to be loaded onto the ship that would carry it to the forward base of Tibbets' 509th Composite Group at Tinian Island in the Marianas. The USS *Indianapolis* had been selected to carry the priceless components because of her speed and size, but for several other reasons she was not an ideal choice. The *Indianapolis* was a heavy cruiser built in 1932; although she was heavily armed, she came from a class of ships that were considered by many experts to be top-heavy and inherently unstable. When shipborne radar equipment was installed on her after Pearl Harbor, it only increased this instability. Another surprising aspect in the choice of the *Indianapolis* was that she had just returned from major repairs after being struck by a Japanese kamikaze aircraft off Okinawa; whilst laid up for repairs, nearly half the ship's company had been replaced and nobody could tell how well both the ship and the crew would operate.

The orders given to Captain McVay, the *Indianapolis*'s commander, were brief and to the point:

> You will sail at high speed to Tinian where your cargo will be taken off by others. You will not be told what the cargo is, but it is to be guarded even after the life of your vessel. If she goes down, save the cargo at all costs, in a lifeboat if necessary. And every day you save

on your voyage will cut the length of the war; by just
that much.

The 15-foot crate containing the gun assembly was bolted to
the deck of the *Indianapolis* and the two escort officers took
the lead-lined bucket containing the uranium 'bullet' to their
cabin, where one of them remained throughout the ten-day
voyage. Despite speculation, the crew of the *Indianapolis*
were unable to discover what they were carrying: most of
them never found out.

Tinian Island, the destination of the *Indianapolis*, was captured by US marines in August 1944. By then, the Japanese
had already constructed three runways and started a fourth;
the Americans took over this work and by the summer of
1945, the four runways at Tinian's North Field comprised
the busiest operational airfield in the world. Twelve miles
long and just over six miles wide at its widest point, in July
1945 Tinian was home to over 20,000 US personnel, living in
tents and prefabricated huts, whilst the jungle and hills of
the centre of the island concealed a dwindling population
of about 500 hidden Japanese soldiers, slowly starving to
death as they attempted to live off the land and the scraps
they could scavenge from American garbage.

The 509th Composite Group began arriving on Tinian at
the end of June. A special fenced-off compound was built
for them, which included a technical workshop where the
final assembly of the bombs would take place. Although
other units on the island were undoubtedly hard pressed,
Tibbets used his protected priority status to ensure that
nothing interfered with his men's training schedule; 509th
aircrews did not take part in bombing missions, 509th
ground crews did not relieve the pressure on the other
overworked mechanics on the island: all hands simply
got on with the job of preparing for their special task

– a task which the majority of them still knew nothing about.

As the 509th ferried their aircraft and personnel into Tinian, the leaders of the alliance that had successfully defeated Nazi Germany were preparing to meet in the German town of Potsdam, a few miles to the south-west of the devastated German capital, Berlin. This was the third major conference of the 'Big Three' leaders, but with the death of Roosevelt in April it was the first one attended by Harry Truman: Stalin and Winston Churchill had now met on several occasions and conceived a wary respect for each other, but Truman was a comparatively unknown quantity. The Potsdam meeting was always going to be different from the previous conferences, at Teheran and Yalta, not least because, with Germany defeated and in ruins, the Allies now had hard decisions to make about policy which could well lead to a split between the Soviet Union and the west. To some extent, the position had been complicated by President Roosevelt's behaviour at Yalta, where, his judgement already clouded by the illness that eventually killed him, he had sought to marginalize Churchill and deal directly with Stalin, a man he thought he could control. In the event, Roosevelt's death had left a weakened Churchill to attempt to guide an inexperienced new US president through their dealings with the wily but paranoid Communist leader. It was, potentially, a recipe for disaster.

One of the principle reasons for calling the conference was to discuss the ways in which the Soviet Union could participate in the war against Japan, but at the same time, it gave an opportunity for Churchill and Truman to discuss the Manhattan Project (or the 'Directorate of Tube Alloys', as it was referred to in Britain). On 17 July, with both leaders in Berlin, news of Trinity had come through from New

Mexico. Churchill was told by Stimson, who was attending the conference as an advisor to Truman:

> On July 17 world-shaking news had arrived. In the afternoon Stimson called at my abode and laid before me a sheet of paper on which was written, 'Babies satisfactorily born.' By his manner I saw something extraordinary had happened. 'It means,' he said, 'that the experiment in the Mexican desert has come off. The atomic bomb is a reality.' Although we had followed this dire quest with every scrap of information imparted to us, we had not been told beforehand, or at any rate I did not know, the date of the decisive trial. No responsible scientist would predict what would happen when the first full-scale atomic explosion was tried. Were these bombs useless or were they annihilating? Now we knew. The 'babies' had been 'satisfactorily born'. No one could yet measure the immediate military consequences of the discovery.

The strategic consequences of this news were enormous, and the next day Churchill and Truman met to consider the implications. Up until this point, when it became clear that the atomic weapons would work, Allied planning had been based on the concept of massive aerial bombardment followed by a seaborne invasion, a rerun in some respects of the D-Day operation in Europe. But for both politicians and soldiers 'Operation Olympic', as the invasion was to be called, was fraught with danger; although General MacArthur, the Supreme Allied Commander, had forecast that the southern Japanese island of Kyushu might be captured with as few as thirty or forty thousand Allied dead, others feared that the toll would be much higher. Winston Churchill believed that:

To quell the Japanese resistance man by man and conquer the country yard by yard might well require the loss of a million American lives and half that number of British – or more if we could get them there.

Although the Americans and British could not be sure that the weapon would bring the war to an end and would therefore have to continue with plans to invade Japan, they were now convinced that they would be able to achieve victory over their enemy without the full-scale participation of the Soviet Union. But they still needed to assuage their qualms about the use of the atomic bombs by offering Japan a way out of the war, to this end they published a declaration on 26 July:

26 July 45

We, the President of the United States, the President of the National Government of the Republic of China, and the Prime Minister of Great Britain, representing the hundreds of millions of our countrymen, have conferred and agree that Japan shall be given an opportunity to end the war.

2. The prodigious land, sea, and air forces of the United States, the British Empire, and China, many times reinforced by their armies and air fleets from the west, are poised to strike the final blows upon Japan. This military power is sustained and inspired by the determination of all the Allied nations to prosecute this war against Japan until she ceases to resist.

3. The result of the futile and senseless German resistance to the might of the aroused free peoples of the world stands forth in awful clarity as an example to the people of Japan. The might that now converges on Japan is immeasurably greater than that which, when applied to the resisting

Nazis, necessarily laid waste the lands, the industry, and the methods of life of the whole German people. The full application of our military power, backed by our resolve, will mean the inevitable and complete destruction of the Japanese forces, and just as inevitably the utter devastation of the Japanese homeland.

4. The time has come for Japan to decide whether she will continue to be controlled by those self-willed militaristic advisors whose unintelligent calculations have brought the Empire of Japan to the threshold of annihilation, or whether she will follow the path of reason.

5. The following are our terms. We shall not deviate from them. There are no alternatives. We shall brook no delay.

6. There must be eliminated for all time the authority and influence of those who have deceived and misled the people of Japan into embarking on world conquest, for we insist that a new order of peace, security and justice will be impossible until irresponsible militarism is driven from the world.

7. Until such a new order is established and until there is convincing proof that Japan's war-making power is destroyed points in Japanese territory designated by the Allies will be occupied to secure the achievement of the basic objectives we are here setting forth.

8. The terms of the Cairo Declaration shall be carried out, and Japanese sovereignty shall be limited to the islands of Honshu, Hokkaido, Kyushu, Shikoku, and such minor islands as we determine.

9. The Japanese forces after being completely disarmed shall be permitted to return to their homes, with the opportunity of leading peaceful and productive lives.

10. We do not intend that the Japanese shall be enslaved as a race nor destroyed as a nation, but stern justice will be meted out to all war criminals, including those who have visited cruelties upon our prisoners. The Japanese

Government shall remove all obstacles to the revival and strengthening of democratic tendencies among the Japanese people. Freedom of speech, of religion, and of thought, as well as respect for fundamental human rights, shall be established.

11. Japan shall be permitted to maintain such industries as will sustain her economy and allow of the exaction of just reparations in kind, but not those industries which would enable her to rearm for war. To this end access to, as distinguished from control of, raw materials shall be permitted. Eventual Japanese participation in world trade relations shall be permitted.

12. The occupying forces of the Allies shall be withdrawn from Japan as soon as these objectives have been accomplished, and there has been established, in accordance with the freely expressed will of the Japanese people, a peacefully inclined and responsible Government.

13. We call upon the Government of Japan to proclaim now the unconditional surrender of all the Japanese Armed Forces, and to provide proper and adequate assurances of their good faith in such action. The alternative for Japan is complete and utter destruction.

The Potsdam Declaration was certainly fair warning for the Japanese government, but without an explicit statement about the power, effects and availability of the atomic bomb, 'complete and utter destruction' had little meaning beyond what their country was already suffering under LeMay's sustained fire-raiding. On the same day that the declaration was issued, the USS *Indianapolis* arrived at Tinian Island to start unloading its deadly cargo, which was destined to change the face of warfare. Not realizing this, the Japanese government, deeply split between militarists who would not contemplate defeat or surrender, and realists who were too weak to enforce their views, rejected the declaration. US Secretary of War Stimson noted:

> In the face of this rejection, we could only proceed to demonstrate that the ultimatum had meant exactly what it said when it stated that if the Japanese continued the war, 'the full application of our military power, backed by our resolve, will mean the inevitable and complete destruction of the Japanese homeland'. For such a purpose the Atomic bomb was an eminently suitable weapon.

Preparations for the bombing were thus to continue.

The *Indianapolis* left Tinian on 26 July, having unloaded its mystery cargo, *en route* for Leyte in the Philippines. There, at last, the crew would have the opportunity for some intensive training before joining the invasion task force for Operation Olympic, which was, by now, being scheduled to take place on 1 November. But on July 29, as the solitary warship cruised through the warm tropical ocean, it passed in front of one of the few remaining Japanese submarines. Unable to believe his luck, the Japanese captain, Lieutenant-Commander Mochitsura Hashimoto, fired a spread of six torpedoes. The range was less than 1,500 yards and most of them hit home; in a series of explosions, ammunition and aviation fuel combined to tear off the bows of the vessel and now, still steaming forwards, the *Indianapolis* took on a vast quantity of water. Within minutes the ship began to heel over and sink, and although the radio officer tried to send a distress signal, all electrical power had been lost after the explosions and he was unable to; Captain McVay's order to abandon ship was passed by word of mouth.

The crew of the USS *Indianapolis* was 1,196 all ranks, of whom approximately 850 managed to escape from the stricken vessel. But their ordeal was not over; negligence at Leyte meant that the *Indianapolis* was not reported overdue, and only when a navy aircraft spotted them by chance was any effort made to resue them. In the end, 96 hours later, 318 survivors were plucked from the Pacific; the rest had either died of their wounds, drowned or, horrifically in the case of 100 or so men, been taken and eaten by sharks. For failing to take adequate anti-submarine countermeasures, Captain McVay was subsequently convicted of negligence at a US navy court martial.

The first operational uranium bomb, nicknamed 'Little Boy', was prepared and ready to go at the end of July. By then, the intense secrecy and security surrounding the 509th within their sealed compound had attracted enough attention for scurrilous attacks by outside personnel; at worst these included attempts by uninformed staff officers to hive off 509th personnel for routine duties – attempts routinely defeated by Tibbets, backed by LeMay if necessary – but there was a lighter side:

Nobody Knows

Into the air the secret rose,
where they're going, nobody knows,
Tomorrow they'll return again,
but we'll never know where they've been.
Don't ask us about results or such,
unless you want to get in Dutch.
But take it from one who is sure of the score,
The 509th is winning the war.

When the other Groups are ready to go,
We have a program of the whole damned show,
And when Halsey's 5th shells Nippon's shore,
Why shucks, we hear about it the day before.

> And MacArthur and Doolittle give out in advance,
> But with this new bunch we haven't a chance.
> We should have been home a month or more,
> For the 509th is winning the war.

But as such attacks continued, crews from the 509th began a series of missions with lone B-29s flying high above Japan dropping single, 10,000-lb 'blockbuster' bombs, partly to accustom the crews to operational conditions and partly to accustom the Japanese to single B-29s causing minimal damage (and thus not being worth attempting to shoot down).

The inexorable progress towards the first operational use of the atomic bomb was taken a step further on 29 July. On that day General Carl Spaatz, who had just been appointed the commanding general of the US Strategic Air Forces in the Pacific, held a meeting at his headquarters in Guam. Present were LeMay, Tibbets, Captain 'Deke' Parsons from Los Alamos, who had come out to supervise the bombs, and two of Spaatz's staff officers. Spaatz had recently caused a minor fracas in Washington DC by insisting to the acting chief of staff of the army that:

> if I'm going to kill 100,000 people I'm not going to do it on verbal orders, I want a piece of paper.

On 29 July, he read out his 'piece of paper':

To: General Carl Spaatz, CG, USASAF:

1. The 509th Composite Group, 20th Air Force, will deliver its first special bomb as soon as weather will permit visual bombing after about 3 August 1945 on one of the targets:

Hiroshima, Kokura, Niigata and Nagasaki. To carry military and civilian scientific personnel from the War Department to observe and record the effects of the explosion of the bomb, additional aircraft will accompany the airplane carrying the bomb. The observing planes will stay several miles distant from the point of impact of the bomb.

2. Additional bombs will be delivered on the above targets as soon as made ready by the project staff. Further instructions will be issued concerning targets other than those listed above.

3. Dissemination of any and all information concerning the use of the weapon against Japan is reserved to the Secretary of War and the President of the United States. No communiques on the subject or releases of information will be issued by commanders in the field without specific prior authority. Any news stories will be sent to the War Department for special clearance.

4. The foregoing directive is issued to you by direction and with the approval of the Secretary of War and of the Chief of Staff, US Army. It is desired that you personally deliver one copy of this directive to General MacArthur and one copy to Admiral Nimitz for their information.

Signed: Thos. T. Handy
General
Acting Chief of Staff

With the order given and the bomb prepared, it was now a question of waiting for the weather.

The plan for the first atomic strike was fairly straight-forward and Tibbets drew it up on the morning of 1 August, even though the final target had not yet been selected. Seven bombers were to take part in the operation, code named 'Centreboard': one, flown by Tibbets, would carry the bomb; two would accompany Tibbets' aircraft to the target in order to film the attack and drop scientific instruments; three would fly to the three potential targets to scout the weather conditions; and the last aircraft would fly to Iwo Jima to act as an alternate strike aircraft in case of malfunction in Tibbets' B-29. When the orders were completed, they were couriered to LeMay on Guam for his final approval. It was LeMay who, on 2 August, confirmed that Hiroshima was to be the primary target. The next day, on the 3rd, he issued the final operation order setting the date for the attack as 6 August and nominating the two alternate targets if Hiroshima could not be bombed: these were to be the Kokura arsenal and the city of Nagasaki. The final preparations now began.

The briefing for the mission took place at 3 p.m. on 4 August. Tibbets assigned roles to his crews: as weather scouts, Captain Claude Eatherley would fly the *Straight Flush* to Hiroshima, Major John Wilson would take *Jabbit III* to Kokura, and Major Ralph Taylor would fly *Full House* to Nagasaki; the two aircraft accompanying Tibbets would be the unnamed B-29 no. 91, flown by Major George Marquardt, and the *Great Artiste*, flown by Major Charles Sweeney; the aircraft going to Iwo Jima as standby would be Captain Charles McKnight's *Top Secret*. Tibbets then introduced Captain 'Deke' Parsons who, resplendent in his naval uniform, was a puzzling presence to the air force men. Parsons' job was to tell them about the weapon:

> The bomb you are about to drop is something new in the history of warfare. It is the most destructive weapon ever produced. We think it will knock out almost everything within a three-mile area.

Parsons ordered the lights dimmed so that he could show a film of the Trinity test; at this moment of tension the projector jammed and then began to chew the film. Parsons recovered his poise:

> The film you are not about to see was made of the only test we have performed. This is what happened. The flash of the explosion was seen for more than ten miles. A soldier 10,000 feet away was knocked off his feet. Another soldier more than five miles away was temporarily blinded. A girl in a town many miles away who had been blind all her life saw a flash of light. The explosion was heard fifty miles away. For those of us who were there, it was the beginning of a new age.

Parsons drew a mushroom shape on a blackboard:

> No one knows exactly what will happen when the bomb is dropped from the air. That has never been done before. But we do expect a cloud this shape will rise to at least 30,000 feet and maybe 60,000 feet, preceded by a flash of light much brighter than the sun's.

In the stunned silence caused by his briefing, Parsons began to hand out polarizing safety goggles to the crews who would be over Hiroshima. Tibbets then resumed the stand, telling the fliers:

> You're now the hottest crews in the airforce. No talking – to anyone. No talking even amongst yourselves. No letters. No writing home. No mentioning of the slightest possibility of a mission.

He proceeded to brief the technical details of the flight: altitude; airspeed; headings; rendezvous; timings. Then he handed over to an air-sea rescue specialist: 'Centreboard' was the most closely supported mission in history: off the coast of Japan a series of Superdumbos – modified B-29s – would be patrolling ready to co-ordinate any rescue mission and fight off opposition, whilst navy flying boats, destroyers, cruisers and submarines would be ready to pick up any crews that ditched. Although they were given the standard briefing on 'conduct after capture' – they were to reveal only their names, ranks, numbers and dates of birth – Tibbets had been secretly issued with a box of cyanide tablets for his crew and had orders to ensure that they should kill themselves to avoid interrogation. He decided to keep this to himself unless capture looked likely.

The briefing was concluded by Tibbets' pep talk.

The next day, after watching the *Great Artiste* drop a dummy bomb to see if the fusing system worked properly – it failed – the final preparations were made. Tibbets sent for a sign painter to name his aircraft, hitherto simply B-29 no. 82. When the painter arrived, Tibbets gave him a slip of paper and told him: 'Paint that on the strike ship, nice and big.' The piece of paper contained the two words 'Enola Gay', Tibbets' mother's forenames: he selected them because she had once told him, during an argument with his father about flying, that he would not be killed.

In the mid-afternoon, the bomb was loaded onto a trolley in the high-security tech area, covered with a tarpaulin and moved out, flanked by a motorcade of military police, to the *Enola Gay*. There it was lowered into a pit and then winched into the aircraft's bomb bay. It was, as yet, not fully armed: although the uranium bullet and target were in place, Parsons had decided not to insert the explosive charge that would fire the bullet until the mission was airborne, hoping that this would reduce the risk of a premature explosion if the heavily loaded bomber crashed on take-off. With the bomb now loaded and the fuel tanks

filled, there was little for the crews to do except eat and try
to sleep.

The final briefing for the mission began a few minutes
into 6 August 1945. Tibbets reminded the crews of their
instructions and told them:

> Do your jobs. Obey your orders. Don't cut corners or take
> chances.

A weather forecaster and a signals officer were then called
forward to make brief announcements and then the group
chaplain was asked to lead the crews in a specially written
prayer:

> Almighty Father, Who wilt hear the prayer of those who love
> Thee, we pray Thee to be with those who brave the heights of
> Thy heaven and who carry the battle to our enemies. Guard
> and protect them, we pray Thee, as they fly their appointed
> rounds. May they, as well as we, know Thy strength and
> power, and armed with Thy might may they bring this
> war to a rapid end. We pray Thee that the end of the war
> may come soon, and that once more we may know peace
> on earth. May the men who fly this night be kept safe in
> Thy care, and may they be returned safely to us. We shall
> go forward trusting in Thee, knowing that we are in Thy
> care now and forever. In the name of Jesus Christ. Amen.

A short while later, trucks arrived to take the crews out to
the aircraft. At about the same time that they were drawing
up to their planes, the three weather scout aircraft took off.
The scene around the *Enola Gay* was bizarre: Groves in
Washington had ordered that film crews and still cameras
should record as much of the mission as possible and so,
immediately prior to one of the most important operations in

military history, the crew of the *Enola Gay* found themselves being treated like movie stars. For a while the airmen basked in the attention, but the necessity of conducting pre-flight checks on their equipment eventually led them all to board. At 2.27 a.m. on 6 August, Tibbets started the engines. At 2.42, Tibbets was told:

Tower to Dimples eight two. Clear for take off.

After making a final check of his instrumentation, Tibbets pushed forward the throttles at 2.45 and *Enola Gay* began to roll down the runway. He held the overloaded plane on the ground long enough for the crew to get slightly panicked, but his take-off was perfect; clear of Tinian, he set course for Iwo Jima under the guidance of Major 'Dutch' van Kirk, the navigator.

Tibbets cruised the aircraft at a height of 4,700 feet towards Iwo Jima where he would rendezvous with his two accompanying planes. As he did so, Captain Parsons, acting as 'weaponeer', began the difficult task of inserting the explosive charge into the bomb; by 3.20 he was finished and, with the exception of the final safety 'plugs', the bomb was now armed and ready for use.

The *Enola Gay* reached the rendezvous at Iwo Jima as dawn was breaking, just before 5 a.m. (Japanese time) and formed up in a loose V formation with the *Great Artiste* and 91. By now many of the aircrafts' crews had fallen asleep, leaving only the essential personnel awake and alert. Major Tom Ferebee, the man who would aim and release the bomb, was dozing in his seat, causing the co-pilot, Captain Robert Lewis, to note:

Our bombardier has been very quiet and methinks he is mentally back in the mid-west part of the old US.

Which was unlikely, Ferebee being a native of North Carolina.

A little way out from Iwo Jima, Tibbets led the formation up to 9,200 feet, where they would stay until the final leg of the approach to Japan. By now, the aircraft were being subjected to the light caress of Japan's early warning radar system, but there was little to be done about it, other than monitor the emissions to ensure that they were not on the same wavelengths as the bomb's proximity fuse radars. A specially trained officer, Lieutenant Jacob Beser, sat in the fuselage doing just that.

At 6.30 a.m., Lieutenant Morris Jeppson, who was assisting Parsons in monitoring the bomb, crawled forward into the bomb bay and removed the safety plugs from the bomb casing; it was now fully armed and ready to go. When this was reported to Tibbets, he eased *Enola Gay* into a climb up to the bombing height of 30,000 feet, switched on the intercom and told the crew:

> We are carrying the world's first atomic bomb. When the bomb is dropped, Lieutenant Beser will record our reactions to what we see. This recording is being made for history. Watch your language and don't clutter up the intercom.

Now they finally knew what they were doing.

Meanwhile, just after 7.09 a.m., *Straight Flush* reached the designated initial point for Tibbets' bombing run over Hiroshima. Looking down from 30,000 feet, Claude Eatherley could see a ten-mile-wide hole in the clouds around the city; conditions were perfect for the bombing. Down below, as he approached the city centre, sirens were wailing, sending the dutiful townspeople scurrying to their shelters. Eatherley ordered his radio operator to send a message directly to *Enola Gay*:

Cloud cover less than 3/10ths at all altitudes. Advice: bomb primary.

Although conditions were equally good at Kokura and Nagasaki, the die was finally cast. Tibbets switched the intercom back on and told his crew:

It's Hiroshima.

As the *Straight Flush* left Japanese airspace, the 'all clear' sounded in Hiroshima and the citizens felt able to breathe a sigh of relief; it was just after 7.30 a.m. and most were on their way to work.

Enola Gay reached its bombing altitude at 7.40 a.m. and ten minutes later achieved landfall to the east of Hiroshima. Now cruising at an equivalent groundspeed of about 325 miles an hour, they made time quickly towards their target. At 8.12 a.m., van Kirk announced that they were at the initial point; at the same time, the aircraft were visually sighted by ground observers based to the east of Hiroshima. As Tibbets steadied the plane for the final approach, a message was being cranked out from a local air defence centre:

8.13 Chugoku Regional Army Reports three large enemy planes spotted, heading west from Saijo. Top Alert.

The final run was the responsibility of Ferebee. According to Tibbets:

Twelve miles from the target, Ferebee called, 'I see it!' He clutched in his bombsight and took control of the plane from me for a visual run.

. . . [he] had the drift well killed but the rate was off a

little. He made two slight corrections. A loud 'blip' on the
radio notified the escort B-29s that the bomb would drop
in two minutes.

After that, Tom looked-up from his bombsight and
nodded to me; it was going to be okay.

He motioned to the radio operator to give the final
warning. A continuous tone went out, telling [the escorts]:
'In fifteen seconds she goes.'

The tone was heard by all the other aircraft on the mission,
including the weather scouts and *Top Secret*, the stand-by
plane on Iwo Jima. Major McKnight, *Top Secret*'s pilot,
told the communication of officer who radioed back to
the 509th:

It's about to drop.

At exactly 8.15:17 a.m., the 'Little Boy' was released from
the bomb bay of the *Enola Gay*. The plane lurched upwards
as the weight of the 9,000 lb bomb ceased to bear on it,
but it still seemed to Ferebee as if the bomb was keeping
pace with them. He watched through the nose as it began
to fall away:

It wobbled a little until it picked up speed, and then it
went right on down just like it was supposed to.

As the bomb left, Tibbets needed to get the *Enola Gay* as
far from the bomb as possible:

I threw off the automatic pilot and hauled Enola Gay into
the turn.

I pulled anti-glare goggles over my eyes. I couldn't see
through them; I was blind. I threw them to the floor.

The bomb continued falling, its in-built radar methodically measuring the distance from the ground as it fell towards the T-shaped Aioi bridge, described by Tibbets as 'the most perfect aiming point I had seen in the whole war'; its outer casing scrawled with messages from the 509th ground crew, including: 'Greetings to the Emperor from the men of the Indianapolis.' At 5,000 feet the barometric safety switch operated and, as the 'Little Boy' reached 1,900 feet, the proximity fuse fired, sending the U235 bullet down the short barrel of the gun assembly into its U235 target. The super-critical mass was formed, drenched in neutrons by the polonium/beryllium initiator, and an uncontrolled chain reaction went through eighty generations before the expanding uranium core was too large to sustain it.

As Tibbets strained to get *Enola Gay* away to the south, 'A bright light filled the plane.' Watching, stunned, from his position in the rear of Enola Gay, Sergeant Bob Caron, the tail gunner, noticed a strange ripple in the air coming towards him. He tried to shout a warning but was too incoherent; the first shock wave hit them. Tibbets was astonished:

> We were eleven and a half miles slant range from the atomic explosion but the whole airplane crackled and crinkled from the blast. I yelled 'Flak!' thinking a heavy gun battery had found us.

Ferebee shouted:

> The sons of bitches are shooting at us!

Caron saw the second shock wave:

> There's another one coming!

Van Kirk thought that the sensation was:

> very much as if you've ever sat on an ash can and had
> somebody hit it with a baseball bat . . . the plane bounced,
> it jumped and there was a noise like a piece of sheet metal
> snapping.

Tibbets realized what was happening:

> Okay. That was the reflected shockwave, bounced back
> from the ground. There won't be any more. It wasn't Flak.
> Stay calm.

Tibbets ordered Beser to start recording the crew's impressions of the blast, starting with Caron, the only one looking directly at the bomb when it exploded:

> A column of smoke is rising fast. It has a fiery red core. A
> bubbling mass, purple grey in colour, with that red core.
> It's all turbulent. Fires are springing up everywhere, like
> flames shooting out of a huge bed of coals. I am starting to
> count the fires. One, two, three, four, five, six . . . fourteen,
> fifteen . . . it's impossible. There are too many to count. Here
> it comes, the mushroom shape that Captain Parsons spoke
> about. It's coming this way. It's like a mass of bubbling
> molasses. The mushroom is spreading out. It's maybe a
> mile or two wide and half a mile high. It's growing up
> and up and up. It's nearly level with us and climbing. It's
> very black, but there is a purplish tint to the cloud. The
> base of the mushroom looks like a heavy undercast that
> is shot through with flames. The city must be below that.
> The flames and smoke are billowing out, whirling out into
> the foothills. The hills are disappearing under the smoke.
> All I can see now of the city is the main dock and what

looks like an airfield. That is still visible. There are planes
down there.

Tibbets remembered:

Lewis pounding my shoulder, saying, 'Look at that! Look
at that! Look at that!' Tom Ferebee wondered about whether
radioactivity would make us all sterile. Lewis said he could
taste atomic fission. He said it tasted like lead.

Watching, Lewis cried out:

My God! Look at that son-of-a-bitch go!

But in the log that he was keeping of the mission, he
wrote:

My God, what have we done?

Captain Parsons handed the radio operator a message form,
for transmission to Tinian; it read:

Clear cut. Successful in all respects. Visible effects greater
than Alamogordo. Conditions normal in airplane following
delivery. Proceeding to base.

Unmolested by Japanese interceptors and anti-aircraft fire,
Enola Gay, the *Great Artiste* and 91 turned for home. They
were 363 miles from Hiroshima when Sergeant Caron
reported that he could no longer see the mushroom cloud.
At 2.58 p.m., just over twelve hours after it had left, Enola
Gay touched down on Tinian. A large crowd of airmen
and officers had gathered on the taxiway, but as the crew
climbed out of the Enola Gay they were held back, creating

Robert Oppenheimer (*left*) and Colonel Leslie Groves beside the remains
of the tower used to set off the world's first atomic explosion on the
Alamogordo bombing range south of Los Alamos. Groves, the army
officer who was placed in charge of the Manhattan Project, was '[the]
biggest sonofabitch I've ever met in my life,' a subordinate remarked, 'but
also one of the most capable individuals.'

Left Robert Oppenheimer, the nuclear physicist who was appointed director of the Los Alamos laboratory. In 1953, he was to be suspended from secret nuclear research because of his alleged left-wing views.

Below Enrico Fermi, the brilliant physicist who built the world's first nuclear reactor, in a squash court at the University of Chicago in 1942. In 1938, Fermi had been awarded the Nobel Prize for physics.

Above General Curtis LeMay, chief of the 21st Bomber Command and the man who issued the order for the attack on Hiroshima.

Below The British connection. *From left to right:* Sir James Chadwick, Britain's 'science ambassador' who discovered the neutron, Leslie Groves, and two American scientists, Richard Tolman and H. D. Smyth. Chadwick was charged with liaison between the British and American atomic development teams.

Left Colonel Paul Tibbets, the brilliant airman who was chosen to lead the first atomic flight over Japan at the age of 29.

This page, right Tibbets at the cockpit of *Enola Gay*, so called after his mother's first names.

Opposite, top The crew of *Enola Gay*.
Opposite, below The B-29 *Enola Gay* returns home after the mission to Hiroshima.

Industrial Promotion Hall
旧産業奨励館

Motoyasu River
元安川

Honkawa River
本川

Honkawa Primary School
本川小学校

Aioi Bridge (T. Bridge)
相生橋（丁字橋）

Koi
己斐町

One month after the atomic blast, Hiroshima is still a city of rubble and ashes. The 'hypocentre' of the air explosion occurred a couple of hundred yards to the left of the wrecked Industrial Promotion Hall (on the left).

Above A sacred Torli gate, one of only a handful of structures in Hiroshima left standing.
Below For days after the explosion, survivors clung to life amid the rubble.

Top left Many who
survived the blast
died soon afterwards
from radiation or
from their wounds.
Hiroshima's authorit
were themselves
overwhelmed.

Top right Bandaged a
in total shock – two
Hiroshima survivors

Left A damaged
clock records the
exact moment that
the second atomic
bomb exploded ove
Nagasaki.

a clearing at the bottom of the ladder. As Tibbets reached the ground, General Spaatz walked up to him, pinned the Distinguished Service Cross on to his flying suit, saluted and walked away without saying a word; it was a signal for the crowd to surge forwards and welcome their heroes home.

5

On the Ground

In 1945 Hiroshima was a city of approximately 320,000 inhabitants, built on the islands and shores of the delta where the river Ota flows into Japan's inland sea. The river breaks up into six main channels which divide the city into islands, linked together by a total of 81 bridges. It is mostly low-lying ground, rarely more than a few feet above sea level, with the exception of a two-hundred-foot-tall hill in the eastern sector of the city; but it is bounded by a natural bowl of hills a little way inland.

The architecture of Hiroshima was varied. For the most part, the inhabitants lived in traditional Japanese wooden houses, and many of the industrial and institutional buildings in the town were made of the same material, but there were some western-style, reinforced-concrete framed constructions, particularly in the town centre, known locally as the 'old town' and housing the governmental and business district. The majority of the town's industrial output was achieved in small, wooden-built workshops and factories set amidst clusters of workers' houses, but Mitsubishi Industries' shipyard was the largest non-military employer in the area.

The largest building in the town centre also lent justification to Hiroshima's selection as the world's first nuclear
target. Hiroshima Castle was four hundred years old and
built on a small, artificial mound, surrounded by a moat.
Inside the keep were the local divisional and regional
headquarters, responsible for the administration of approximately 40,000 soldiers in Hiroshima alone; the military
district around it also housed a training depot, a hospital,
an ammunition dump and a supply area. Underneath the
castle was a civil defence headquarters, ready to direct
anti-aircraft fire in the event of a raid.

Also in Hiroshima, positioned in a suburb of the town
beneath Mount Futaba, was the headquarters of the Japanese
2nd Army, under the command of Field Marshal Shunruko
Hata, who had been given responsibility for the ground
defence of southern Japan against the forthcoming Allied
invasion. Hata's previous career had encompassed the
Russo-Japanese war of 1905, a period as military attaché
to Germany and delegate to the Paris peace conference of
1919, a stint as minister of war in 1939, and personal rule
over Japanese-occupied China from 1941 to 1944. In April
1945, Hata had been a possible candidate to succeed as prime
minister, but instead he had been nominated to mobilize the
population of southern Japan in defence of their homeland.
To this end, women and children were being taught to use
pikes, spears and petrol bombs, and the sick, disabled and
bedridden were set to work constructing booby traps for
use against the invaders. Despite this, Hata was under no
illusions that Japan was still capable of defeating America
and the Allies; instead, he hoped that Japan might make
better terms than the unconditional surrender that was then
being demanded.

As the war had continued, so Japan had been forced
more and more to involve the whole population in the war

effort. Notwithstanding Field Marshal Hata's rudimentary training in defensive techniques, the population were also widely involved in the construction of war *materiel* and in civil defence measures. In Hiroshima, the most visible aspect of this was the construction, in the town, of a number of enormous firebreaks, made by the simple expedient of demolishing swathes of wooden buildings and clearing the rubble of any combustible material. It had become clear, since the American firestorm raid on Tokyo in March, that Japanese building methods rendered their towns and cities particularly vulnerable to incendiary attack.

In Hiroshima, with the adult population already stretched to the limit by the demands of war industries, the government mobilized children for the demolition work. Teenagers were brought back to the city from the surrounding countryside, to which they had been evacuated, and began a routine which combined education with hard physical labour. The government had, in any case, decided to keep all schools open during the summer of 1945 so that parents, without the burdens of child care, would be able to put in longer hours at work. As a result, children from five years of age upwards were at the many schools dotted throughout the city.

But despite the extensive precautions that were being taken in the city, up to the morning of 6 August 1945, Hiroshima had not been subjected to extensive air attack. On 30 April, a lone B-29 had dropped its cargo of ten 500-lb bombs, having failed to find its target at nearby Kure harbour: ten people were killed and another thirty or so injured. On 28 July, two B-24s had caused considerable excitement when they had overflown the anti-aircraft batteries to the south of Hiroshima and been shot down. The surviving American airmen had been hunted down by Kempei Tai security policemen and taken to Hiroshima

Castle for interrogation. The lack of air raids had spawned some bizarre rumours in the town; these included the suggestion that President Truman's mother was a prisoner at Hiroshima Castle, having been there when war was declared, and even that:

> Truman's mother is from Hiroshima! That is why we have not been bombed. She has told her son to spare this one city in all Japan!

So a Japanese anti-aircraft officer told one of his subordinates. Unfortunately, the truth was more prosaic; General LeMay's B-29s had simply not got around to attacking Hiroshima by the time the city was reserved as a possible atomic target.

Thus, despite the desperation of Japan's war situation, 6 August 1945 started as a day like any other for the citizens of Hiroshima. The United States' Strategic Bombing Survey subsequently noted that the morning was:

> clear, with a few clouds at high altitude. Wind was from the south with a velocity of about 4.5 miles an hour. Visibility was 10 to 15 miles.

Whilst, on the ground, Dr Michihiko Hachiya thought that:

> The hour was early, the morning still, warm and beautiful . . . shimmering leaves, reflecting sunlight from a cloudless sky, made a pleasant contrast with the shadows in my garden.

At 7.09 a.m., the civil defence control centre called an air-raid alert when a single B-29 was detected in the area

– it was Captain Eatherly in *Straight Flush* acting as weather scout for the *Enola Gay* – but as the plane departed, the alert was cancelled and the all clear announced. As a result, the citizens of the town left the relative safety of their air-raid shelters and resumed their tasks:

> the siren sounded the all-clear. You could say that it was the sound of this siren that killed the great majority of the citizens of Hiroshima.
>
> (Susumu Kimura, schoolgirl)

On the parade ground of Hiroshima Castle soldiers resumed their morning PT; on the buses and trams in the city, commuters continued their journeys to work; the schoolchildren continued demolishing houses. As the clock ticked toward 8.15 nobody was too concerned about the approach of three more American aircraft:

> We were so used to observation flights of B-29s that at first we hardly paid any attention to this one. However, when the engine hum changed to a shrill whine we instinctively looked up at the sky. One B-29, bathed in the direct rays of the midsummer sun, gives off a dazzling gleam from its mighty flank, and leaving a fleecy white cloud-trail across the blue sky, has just completed a sharp turn and goes climbing upward with a terrific roar.
>
> (Tetsuo Miyata, teacher's assistant)

Tibbets had thrown the *Enola Gay* into its evasive manoeuvre.

> I saw a single enemy airplane flying over Hiroshima. It dropped or fired a brilliant object. I thought at first it was an incendiary bomb . . .
>
> (Kure dockyard worker)

Many who saw the measuring instruments drop from the *Straight Flush* noticed the parachute open above them and assumed that the crew were bailing out, but then:

> A flame appeared that was even brighter than the sun. I thought I might get hurt so I fell flat on the ground.
>
>   (Kure dockyard worker)

> My little brother had just put out his hand to catch [a] red dragon-fly when, in that instant, there was a flash and with my whole body I received a shock as if I had been thrown into a furnace.
>
>   (Shintaro Fukuhara, schoolboy)

> As I was about to enter the office, I saw through an open window what looked like a golden lightning flash that had blown up out of the earth. The weird light was everywhere. I immediately thought of the air raid and hurled myself prostrate in the passage.
>
>   (Kenshi Hirata, accountant)

The flash and the 'weird, golden light' were accompanied, as at Trinity, by an instantaneous heat pulse:

> Its duration was probably less than one tenth of a second and its intensity sufficient to cause nearby flammable objects . . . to burst into flame and to char poles as far as 4,000 yards away from the hypocenter . . . At 600–700 yards it was sufficient to chip and roughen granite . . . the heat also produced bubbling of tile to about 1,300 yards.
>
>   (US Strategic Bombing Survey)

Witnesses say that people who were directly under the explosion in the open had their exposed skin burnt so severely that it was immediately charred brown or black:

these people died within minutes or at most hours. Both in Hiroshima and Nagasaki, burns on exposed skin were very severe up to about 1,500 yards from the centre of the damage. At this distance, some escaped with less severe burns, although very severe burns were occasionally reported at nearly 1½ miles from the centre of damage. Mild burns extended to distances of 2½ miles and more. Stories that white people were unharmed in Hiroshima where the darker skinned Japanese received fatal burns were not substantiated.

(British Mission Report)

Within one mile of ground zero, the heat was sufficient to cause . . . 'not only carbonization but also evaporation of the viscera' in humans; in other words, the heat caused the soft internal organs of the victims simply to boil away, whilst their bones became brittle sticks of charcoal. Another grotesque effect of the heat flash was noted by the British mission to Hiroshima and Nagasaki in November 1945; this was that darker-coloured clothing would char at much greater distances than light colours. Examples of this included:

A white cotton blouse, the pale pink sleeves of which were patterned with small sprays, each about a ³⁄₁₆ inch in diameter, of green leaves and red flowers. This blouse had been worn in the open well over a mile from the center of damage, and was unscorched; except that over an area on the left shoulder the sprays had burnt out and left holes.

This comparatively dispassionate account neglects to mention the corresponding damage to the skin beneath the blouse.

The US Strategic Bombing Survey noted that:

The large majority of people within 3000 feet of ground zero were killed immediately ... Persons in the open were burned on exposed surfaces, and within 3000–5000 feet many were burned to death. In many instances clothing burst into flame and had to be beaten out ...

Little Boy's heat flash caused the instantaneous deaths of thousands of humans and mortal wounding to thousands more:

My little brother was burned on his face and hands and his face was all swollen. He was just three. He was a cute little brother but he died after a week.
He died calling, 'Mummy! Mummy!'
(Ruriko Araoka, aged 5 in 1945)

And at the same time as the people were dying, pet dogs and cats, birds, snakes, spiders, rats and rabbits 'crackled and were gone'. In many cases, they left behind strange shadows where their bodies had shielded the surfaces of roads and buildings from the charring effect of the flash. Those who were not destined to die from flash burns had, in many cases, the most appalling injuries from them nevertheless. Michihiko Hachiya:

asked Dr Koyama what his findings had been in patients with eye injuries.
'Those who watched the plane had their eye grounds burned,' he replied. 'The flash of light apparently went through the pupils and left them with a blind area in the central portion of their visual fields.

'Most of the eye-ground burns are third degree, so cure is impossible.'

Among those killed by the heat flash were several members of the crews of the B-24s that had been shot down over the city the previous week. Nevertheless, flash burns were only to account for the deaths of some 20–30 per cent of the immediate casualties of the bomb.

For a few seconds after the heat flash passed over them, the people of Hiroshima could have been forgiven for thinking that the worst was over, but in its wake came an even more devastating effect of the cataclysmic chain reaction: the shock wave.

The TNT equivalent 'yield' of the Hiroshima bomb has been variously estimated but, in all probability, the most likely figure is around 12,500 tons. The British investigatory commission in November 1945 tried to make sense of this concept:

an explosion of 20,000 tons of TNT would be expected to cause at a distance of about ½ mile from the centre of damage an instantaneous pressure rise of about 10 lb per square inch, falling back to atmospheric pressure in about ½ second: and since, during part of this time, there would be a wind of the order of 500 miles an hour, the pressure initially imposed on parts of a building might be as high as 30 lb per square inch. Such figures could be multiplied and become meaningless: the reader who finds them so may prefer a summary analogy. This is that the scale of destruction expected would be that which would befall a model town built to the scale of Gulliver's Lilliput, 1 inch to the foot, if there were exploded above it a bomb more than twice as large as the largest British 'Blockbuster', which with its case weighed about six tons.

According to the US Strategic Bombing Survey:

> Within a radius of 7000 feet almost every Japanese house col-
> lapsed and others received serious structural damage . . .

Along with the structural damage, of course, went the
effects on the human inhabitants of the city:

> I saw what seemed like an incendiary bomb exploding to
> the rear of the plane (in the sky to the south). It was
> followed by a flash (1 to 2 seconds duration). Thinking
> it was an incendiary bomb, I started to take shelter in
> the station building but had only gone a few steps when
> I felt a tremendous concussion strike me from behind. I
> immediately fell to the ground and covered my face . . .
>
> (Kure dockyard worker)

> I felt as though I had been struck on the back with something
> like a big hammer, and thrown into boiling oil . . . I seem
> to have been blown a good way to the north, and I felt as
> though the directions were all changed around . . .
>
> (Schoolgirl)

The blast wave, as it flattened the city, threw up an immense
cloud of dust and dirt:

> When I opened my eyes after being blown at least eight
> yards, it was as dark as though I had come up against a
> black-painted fence . . . The first thing that my eyes lighted
> upon then was the flat stretch of land with only dust clouds
> rising from it. Everything had crumbled away in that one
> moment, and changed into streets of rubble, street after
> street of ruins.
>
> (Schoolboy)

When I opened my eyes, I couldn't see a thing. It was as if it had suddenly become midnight in the heat of day . . .

(Tsutomu Yamaguchi, ship designer)

The British study observed three particular differences between the blast effects of conventional bombs and those at Hiroshima:

Mass Distortion – It is usual for a bomb to damage only a part of a large building, which may then collapse further under the action of gravity. The blast wave from the atomic bomb, however, was so large that it damaged whole buildings, pushing them askew . . . The effect, which occurred with all types of buildings, resembles damage done by wind, and operates somewhat in the same way . . .

Infrequency of Blast Suction – After the blast pressure has fallen from its peak back to zero, there always follows a period of suction. Although this suction is weaker than the original pressure, it lasts several times as long, and therefore normally does much damage to objects which had no time to fail under the usually brief initial pressure. Pressures from the atomic bomb however lasted long enough to give windows, doors, walls, and even chimneys and telegraph poles time to fail. As a result, effects which could be ascribed to blast suction were unusually scarce, although a few were observed in Hiroshima.

Downward Thrust – Because the explosion was high in the air, much of the damage was due to downward pressure. Most characteristic was the 'dishing' of the flat roof slabs of reinforced concrete buildings, some of which assumed a saucer shape. For the same reason, telegraph and other poles remained upright immediately below the explosion, but were overturned or tilted at greater distances from the centre of damage. Trees below the explosion remained upright, but had their branches torn downward.

As far as the inhabitants were concerned, a second effect of the blast wave was that they were showered with huge quantities of glass, rubble and other mobile fragments of the city, often at extremely high velocity. The US Strategic bombing survey observed that:

> Apparently there were comparatively few instances of legs and arms being torn from the body by flying debris.

But Dr Hachiya, finding himself trapped in the rubble of his own house, found that he was obliged to go through the ruin of his neighbour's:

> so through the house we went – running, stumbling, falling, and then running again until in headlong fight we tripped over something and fell sprawling into the street. Getting to my feet, I discovered that I had tripped over a man's head.

An engineer noticed in his workplace that:

> All the glass that had been in one side of the house was imbedded deeply, in spears, in the opposite wall.

But the blast turned the most innocuous substances into agents of pain and horror:

> I had never seen such a horrifying sight as those five shivering boys. Blood was pouring in streams from deep cuts all over their bodies, mingling with their perspiration, and their skin was burned deep red, like the colour of cooked

lobsters. At first it seemed, strangely, that their burned and lacerated backs and chests were growing green grass! Then I saw that hundreds of blades of sharp grass had been driven deep into their flesh, evidently by the force of the blast.

(Tsutomu Yamaguchi)

The effect of the blast on those burnt and blistered by the flash was appalling; it literally tore their loosened skin off.

In the wake of the heat flash and the blast wave came fire, caused partly by the direct radiated heat from the bomb, partly by other causes – gas leaks, electrical sparking and so forth. The British study examined the causes:

The Mission was most impressed by the accumulation of indirect evidence from the many reinforced concrete buildings the basements, the stairs or some floors of which had been screened and contained no fire when floors of the same building with windows exposed to the flash were gutted by fire. A number of reinforced concrete buildings in Hiroshima with shuttered windows escaped fire, apparently because the heat radiation, travelling at the speed of light, had arrived and died away before the blast, travelling only a few thousand feet per second, blew out the shutters to expose the interior. The dense surrounding fires did not spread to these buildings . . .

Indirect causes undoubtedly produced many fires. Braziers, widely used in industry as well as in the home, must have started some: some will have begun at gas leaks; and the primitive electrical wiring no doubt started others, however rapid was the circuit breaking system . . . experience has shown that the danger of indirect fires always exists in large scale bombing, in every part of the world . . .

It is certain that firespread did occur [in Hiroshima]; but more striking is the evidence for vast numbers of

separate points of fire, which made fire-fighting among
these combustible buildings hopeless from the outset.

. . . both direct and indirect fires must be regarded
as active dangers from atomic bombs. Indeed, whether
radiated heat is or is not an important cause of fire, the
high temperatures produced by it plainly create conditions
exceptionally favourable to the emergence and continuance
of serious fires, however caused. For example, the debris of
demolished Japanese houses beyond the fire zone which was
examined in Hiroshima would rarely have supported fire at
ordinary temperatures. Yet it must have been debris in this
state which burnt there for days, presumably as a result of
the initial drying and scorching by the bomb.

But these dry phrases fail to conjure up the nightmare that
was now faced by the wounded who had survived the flash
and the blast but who were trapped in the rubble of the
devastated city. Yamaguchi, the ship designer, was about
one and a half miles from ground zero:

As the dust blew away and my surroundings became visible,
I saw what seemed to be thousands of tiny, flickering lamps
all over the street and in the fields. They were little circles of
flame, each about the size of a doughnut. Myriads of them
were hanging on the leaves of the potato plants.

Air rushing in to feed the flames of these many fires caused
a firestorm to develop. As was noted by the British survey,
fires burnt with an unusual ferocity and thoroughness and
many injured burnt to death, unable to escape them.
Survivors became frantic in the struggle to get away from
the flames and this created its own series of tragedies:

As I went further, I came upon a reservoir used for the

prevention of fire. In the reservoir there were numberless corpses piled one upon another. It was a hill of dead bodies in green. All of these people must have jumped into the reservoir because of the heat.

(Kenshi Hirata)

At the moment that the bomb detonated over Hiroshima, it is thought that there may have been about 320,000 people present in the city. The heat flash, the blast wave and the subsequent fires probably accounted for 80,000 of them in the first few hours, but those that survived were, as the Los Alamos scientists thought, in a 'new world':

Although I knew the city well, it was actually difficult to find my way, for all the familiar landmarks had gone, and the streets I had often walked were now buried in debris and ashes.

(Kenshi Hirata)

The survivors were now faced with the problem of trying to avoid the flames and go to the aid of friends, family, loved ones and strangers; or simply to escape:

The whole city was burning. Black smoke was billowing up and we could hear the sound of big things exploding . . . The fires were burning. There was a strange smell all over. Blue-green balls of fire were drifting around. I had a terrible lonely feeling that everybody else in the world was dead and only we were left alive.

(Schoolgirl)

I was determined not to escape without my mother. But the flames were steadily spreading and my clothes were already on fire and I couldn't stand it any longer. So screaming,

'Mummy, Mummy!' I ran wildly into the middle of the flames. No matter how far I went it was a sea of fire all around and there was no way to escape. So beside myself I jumped into our water tank. The sparks were falling everywhere so I put a piece of tin over my head to keep out the fire. The water in the tank was hot like a bath. Beside me there were four or five other people who were all calling someone's name. While I was in the water tank everything became like a dream and sometime or other I became unconscious . . . Five days after that I learned that mother had finally died just as I had left her.

(Schoolgirl)

I left my mother there and went off . . . I was later told by a neighbour that my mother had been found dead, face down in a water tank . . . very close to the spot where I had left her . . . If I had been a little older or stronger I could have rescued her . . . Even now I still hear my mother's voice calling me to help her.

(Schoolgirl)

There were numberless injured persons all around me, lying on the ground, some held down by fallen timbers, all screaming and shouting for help. I saw that they were all still alive, but horribly injured. Many looked like ghosts, with the skin peeled off their faces and hanging down over their shoulders like thin silk pennants. All those who had been facing in the direction of the blast had their exposed skin torn off in a thick layer which had blown back. The sight left me numb with horror.

(Kite maker)

As I continued to search for my wife along the banks of the river, I saw more corpses at the foot of a bridge, damming the water.

(Accountant)

We went up the slope of the hill at Koi and looked around, there were indeed some students from Prefectural Girls' High there but my sister was nowhere to be seen.

The next day we hunted for her in the same way, far and wide. The students at the river's edge who yesterday had been rather hopeful – today they could not say a word and just looked at us in appealing recognition. Many of them who had still been alive yesterday were now dead. As we were about to leave there, they said in small, faint voices, 'Sayonara . . .'

It was hard for us to leave them. The next day when we went there those students were all dead.

(Schoolgirl)

A little farther on there was a woman lying with a big log fallen across her legs so that she couldn't get away.

When father saw that he shouted, 'Please come and help!'

But not a single person came to help. They were all too intent on saving themselves.

Finally father lost his patience, and shouting, 'Are you all Japanese or not?', he took a rusty saw and cut off her leg and rescued her.

(Schoolgirl)

I felt almost ashamed, because I wasn't hurt myself.

(Schoolgirl)

I remember a baby playing alone by the side of the river, surrounded by fire and smoke, and I've often wondered how it escaped injury.

(Labourer)

The first [casualty that I saw] was a little boy. He was completely naked, his skin was all peeled off as if he had been flayed, and the nails were falling from the ends of his fingers. His flesh was all deep red. When I first saw him I wasn't sure that I was looking at a human being.

(Accountant)

I found the aid station surrounded by dead bodies, or should I say 'charred' bodies, for I had no way of telling whether the unfortunate people were alive or dead.

(Ship designer)

On both sides of the road, bedding and pieces of cloth had been carried out and on these were lying people who had been burned to a reddish-black colour and whose entire bodies were frightfully swollen. Making their way among them are three high school girls who looked as though they are from our school; their faces and everything were completely burned and they held their arms out in front of their chests like kangaroos with only their hands pointed downward; from their whole bodies something like thin paper is dangling – it is their peeled off skin which hangs there, and trailing behind them the unburned remnants of their puttees, they stagger exactly like sleepwalkers.

(Schoolgirl)

The people passing along the street are covered with blood and trailing the rags of their torn clothes after them. The skin of their arms is peeling off and dangling from their finger tips, and they go walking silently, hanging their arms before them.

(Schoolgirl)

On the broad street in the Hakushima district, naked burned cadavers are particularly numerous. Among them are the wounded who are still alive. A few have crawled under the burned-out autos and trams. Frightfully injured forms beckon to us and then collapse.

(German Jesuit missionary)

I had the feeling that all the human beings on the face of the earth had been killed off and only the five of us were left behind in an uncanny world of the dead . . . I saw several people plunging their heads into a half broken water tank and drinking the water . . . When I was close enough to see inside the tank I said 'Oh!' out loud and instinctively drew back. What I had seen in the tank were the faces of monsters reflected from the water died red with blood. They had clung to the side of the tank and plunged their heads in to drink and there in that position they had died. From their burned and tattered middy blouses I could tell that they were high school girls, but there was not a hair left on their heads; the broken skin of their burned faces was stained bright red with blood. I could hardly believe that these were human faces.

(Schoolboy)

Streetcars were standing at Kawaya-Cho and Kamiya-Cho and inside were dozens of bodies, blackened beyond recognition. I saw fire reservoirs filled to the brim with dead people who looked as though they had been boiled alive . . . In one reservoir there were so many dead people there wasn't enough room for them to fall over. They must have died sitting in the water.

(Doctor)

We were still in the river by evening and it got cold. No matter where you looked there was nothing but burned people all around.

(Schoolgirl)

As I came to the river and went down the bank to the water, I found that the stream was filled with dead bodies. I started to cross by crawling over the corpses, on my hands and knees. As I got about a third of the way across, a dead

body began to sink under my weight and I went into the
water, wetting my burned skin. It pained severely. I could
go no further, as there was a break in my bridge of corpses,
so I turned back to the shore.

(Ship designer)

In a discussion of the relative importance as causes of
death of the various lethal factors, the British Mission
observed that:

with the Atomic, as with other bombs, indirect injuries
caused the death of a high proportion of the casualties,
and probably of the bulk of them – except in so far as
these were killed as it were several times over, by each
lethal agent separately.

Compared to the human suffering, the physical damage to
the City seems almost irrelevant, but of course it represented
an additional misery to the population. Of the 76,000 buildings in the city, 48,000 were completely destroyed, whilst
most public utilities and services were wrecked. The direct
result of the damage was that the people of Hiroshima were
unable to help themselves, particularly as unseasonable bad
weather brought a black rain of dust onto the town. The US
Strategic Bombing Survey reported that:

Those who were able made a mass exodus from the city
into the outlying hills. There was no organised activity.
The people appeared stunned by the catastrophe and
rushed about as jungle animals suddenly released from
a cage.

But even as outside relief began to arrive in the town in

the days after the explosion, a further horror appeared to strike down those who thought that they had survived the bomb: radiation sickness. The British study observed that:

The gamma rays were very penetrating and passed through the skin without affecting it. As a result, those exposed to gamma rays, if they were protected from flashburn and from indirect injury, showed no immediate ill-effect. Even those severely irradiated probably did not show the characteristic symptoms, nausea, vomiting and fever, for 24 hours, and rarely died in less than one week. These symptoms were followed by bloody diarrhoea, occurring most frequently in the second week, at which time loss of appetite and general malaise also became marked. Patients begin to lose their hair after the first week.

Thereafter, in the severe cases, the clinical picture came to be dominated by signs of deficient blood formation. This effect on the blood is indirect, and therefore delayed: the gamma rays do not attack the cells in the bloodstream, but the primitive cells in the bone marrow, from which most of the different types of cells in the blood are formed. Therefore serious effects begin to appear only as the fully-formed cells already in the blood die off gradually and are not replaced as they would be normally by new cells formed in the bone marrow. In severe cases, it was apparent that the gamma rays had virtually killed the entire bone marrow. In such cases, all three types of cells formed in the marrow became deficient: red cells, platelets, and white cells. As red cell formation ceased, the patient began to suffer from progressive anaemia. As platelet formation ceased, the thin blood seeped in small and large haemorrhages into the skin and the retina of the eye, and sometimes into the intestines and the kidneys. The fall in the number of white cells, which was useful in diagnosing mild cases because it could be detected by taking blood counts, in severe cases lowered resistance, so that the patient inevitably fell prey to some infection, usually spreading from the mouth and accompanied by gangrene of the lips, the tongue, and sometimes the throat. Death in these cases was the result of a combination of anaemia, internal bleeding, and infection. Deaths probably began in about a week after the explosion, reached a peak in about three weeks, and had for the most part ceased after six to eight weeks.

The distances at which these effects were felt are not easy to determine. It is thought that gamma rays ultimately caused the death of everyone who was fully exposed to them up to a distance of ½ mile from the centre of damage. A figure can be obtained for the 50 per cent chance of survival, from the evidence of two groups of workers who had been brought into Hiroshima from an outlying village, and who were working in the open but screened by wooden buildings at 1,200 yards from the centre of damage. Of the total of 198 men, 6 were killed immediately by the debris and 95 subsequently died, it is believed all from the effects of gamma rays. Allowing for some small protection afforded by the wooden buildings, it is estimated that people in the open have a 50 per cent chance of surviving the effects of gamma radiation at ¾ mile from the centre of damage. As regards lesser effects, loss of hair was recorded up to 1¼ miles from the centre of damage, and some doctors felt that the milder forms of radiation sickness, more difficult to diagnose, may have extended to 2 miles.

The US Strategic Bombing Survey reported that:

All or nearly all pregnant women in various stages of pregnancy who survived and who had been within 3,000 feet of the centre of the explosion have had miscarriages or premature infants who died shortly after birth.

And that:

Sperm counts done in Hiroshima by the Joint Commission have revealed low sperm counts or complete aspermia for as long as 3 months afterwards in males who were within 5,000 feet of the centre of the explosion.

But those who had to experience it were less matter-of-fact:

We were being killed against our will by something completely unknown to us . . . It is the misery of being thrown into a world of new terror and fear, a world more unknown than that of people sick with cancer.

(Writer)

Mother was completely bedridden. The hair of her head had almost all fallen out, her chest was festering, and from the two-inch hole in her back a lot of maggots were crawling in and out. The place was full of flies and mosquitoes and fleas, and an awfully bad smell hung over everything. Everywhere I looked there were many people like this who couldn't move. From the evening when we arrived Mother's condition got worse and we seemed to see her weakening before our eyes. Because all night long she was having trouble breathing, we did everything we could to relieve her. The next morning Grandmother and I fixed some gruel. As we took it to Mother, she breathed her last breath. When we thought she had stopped breathing altogether, she took one last deep breath and did not breathe any more after that. This was nine o'clock in the morning of the 19th of

August. At the site of the Japan Red Cross Hospital, the smell of the bodies being cremated is overpowering. Too much sorrow makes me like a stranger to myself, and yet despite my grief I cannot cry.

6

The Aftermath

The first that the outside world heard of the destruction of Hiroshima came from official statements issued by the governments of the United States and Britain; the blow that had fallen on Japan was so shattering and incomprehensible that it took some days for the Japanese government to appreciate quite what had happened. President Truman was travelling back from the Potsdam conference aboard the USS *Augusta* when he was told the news; he told sailors in the mess deck where he was dining that 'This is the greatest thing that has ever happened.' His official statement, prepared prior to the bombing, was issued from Washington DC on 6 August: with the Japanese still fighting, it was more a warning to their government:

> We spent $2,000,000,000 on the greatest scientific gamble in history – and won.
> . We shall destroy their docks, their factories, and their communications. Let there be no mistake: we shall completely destroy Japan's power to make war.
> If they do not now accept our terms they may expect a

rain of ruin from the air the like of which has never been seen on this earth.

Britain, the junior partner in the enterprise, also issued a statement. In a shock result, the government of Winston Churchill had been defeated in the general election held in July, and the new British prime minister was Clement Attlee, leading a government of the Labour Party. Barely through the front door of 10 Downing Street, Attlee contented himself with releasing a statement that had been drafted by Churchill:

> It is now for Japan to realise, in the glare of the first atomic bomb that has smitten her, what the consequences will be of an indefinite continuance of this terrible means of maintaining a rule of law in the world.
>
> This revelation of the secrets of nature, long mercifully withheld from man, should arouse the most solemn reflections in the mind and conscience of every human capable of comprehension. We must indeed pray that these awful agencies will be made to conduce to peace amongst nations, and that instead of wreaking measureless havoc upon the entire globe they may become a perennial fountain of prosperity.

Although Churchill made the point that British science had been a significant contributor to the project, he acknowledged American leadership:

> The whole burden of execution, including the setting up of the plants and many technical processes connected therewith in the practical sphere, constitutes one of the greatest triumphs of American – or indeed human – genius of which there is record.

The American and British statements, prepared before the bombing, contained no details of damage – none were available – and it is a feature of survivors' accounts that they could hear American planes flying above them all day as the Allies attempted to find out how well the bomb had worked. All the newspapers could do was relay further official statements:

Washington Aug 6 – The US War Dept announced tonight that an impenetrable cloud of dust and smoke had covered the target area after the bomb had been dropped at Hiroshima. This made accurate reports of the damage impossible at present.

Despite this, it was clear from the effects seen from the *Enola Gay* and the observer aircraft that colossal damage and loss of life had been achieved. At the Los Alamos laboratory, Otto Frisch was working when:

some three weeks after Alamogordo, there was a sudden noise in the laboratory, of running footsteps and yelling voices. Somebody opened my door and shouted 'Hiroshima has been destroyed!'; about a hundred thousand people were thought to have been killed. I still remember the feeling of unease, indeed nausea, when I saw how many of my friends were rushing to the telephone to book tables at the La Fonda hotel in Santa Fé, in order to celebrate.

That same evening at Los Alamos, Oppenheimer made a speech in the auditorium, after walking through a cheering crowd of scientists pumping his fists in the air, during which he told his audience, according to one observer:

It was too early to determine what the results of the bombing might have been, but he was sure that the Japanese didn't like it . . . He was proud, and he showed it, of what he had accomplished . . . And his only regret was that we hadn't developed the bomb in time to have it used against the Germans. This practically raised the roof.

But later the same evening, Oppenheimer began to face reality when he saw one of his scientists throwing up into the bushes outside the lecture theatre.

At their secret prison outside Cambridge in England the German atomic scientists were shocked and amazed, both at the fact that the Allies had been able to develop a bomb, and that it had been used. Their conversations were being secretly recorded by British intelligence:

Hahn: . . . If the Americans have a uranium bomb then you're all second raters. Poor old Heisenberg.

Laue: The innocent!

Heisenberg: Did they use the word uranium in connection with this atomic bomb?

All: No.

Heisenberg: Then it's got nothing to do with atoms, but the equivalent of 20,000 tons of high explosive is terrific . . . All I can suggest is that some dilettante in America who knows very little about it has bluffed them in saying 'If you drop this it has the equivalent of 20,000 tons of high explosive' and in reality it doesn't work at all.

Hahn: At any rate Heisenberg you're just second raters and you may as well pack up.

Heisenberg: I quite agree.

A little later, Otto Hahn, the discoverer of fission, was speaking to Professor Gerlach, who had led the German uranium research effort:

Hahn: Are you upset because we did not make the uranium bomb? I thank God on my bended knees that we did not make a uranium bomb.

By 8 August, the Japanese began to react officially. An official statement broadcast from Tokyo claimed that use of the atomic bomb was:

sufficient to brand the enemy for ages to come as the destroyer of mankind and as public enemy no. 1 of social justice.

But this rather bizarre propaganda should be contrasted with a rather more sober description of what actually happened which was broadcast on Radio Tokyo the same day:

The impact of the bomb was so terrific that practically all living things, human and animal, were literally seared to death by the tremendous heat and pressure engendered by the blast. All the dead and injured were burned beyond recognition. With houses and buildings crushed, including many emergency medical facilities, authorities are having their hands full in giving every available relief possible under the circumstances. The effect of the bomb is widespread. Those outdoors burned to death, while those indoors were killed by the indescribable pressure and heat.

The news of Hiroshima that was starting to percolate through to Tokyo in the days after the attack precipitated the 'realist' elements of the government into action. With the Soviet Union still neutral, the Japanese foreign ministry was desperate to use their good offices to open negotiations with the Allies. The bombing of Hiroshima added increased impetus to their efforts. But when, at 5 p.m. on 8 August, the Japanese ambassador to the Soviets finally managed to meet Molotov, the Soviet foreign minister, it was simply to be told that the Soviet Union was declaring war on Japan as from midnight.

On the same afternoon that Ambassador Sato met Molotov in Moscow, Major Chuck Sweeney was flying his plane *the Great Artiste* off the coast of Tinian. On board was a dummy plutonium implosion bomb, fully equipped with the various electronic components necessary to detonate the bomb at the correct height and cause the spherical detonation wave to implode the plutonium core to a super-critical density around the neutron initiator. The only part missing was the core itself. At a predetermined position he released the weapon, and scientists in the 509th tech area monitored its fall into the Pacific. The bomb worked perfectly: the barometric and proximity switches functioned at precisely the right moment and the sophisticated instantaneous detonation unit fired correctly. Commander Frederick Ashworth, acting as nanny to the plutonium bomb just as 'Deke' Parsons had looked after the uranium weapon, now knew that the second atomic mission – to bomb the Kokura arsenal – would go ahead as planned the next day.

In the meantime, a massive propaganda effort was being organized to try to bring pressure to bear on the split Japanese government to bring an end to the war. A message was worked out and broadcast to Japan from various US propaganda stations based around the Pacific; at the same time, the text was printed onto 6,000,000 leaflets for air-dropping over the Empire. It read:

TO THE JAPANESE PEOPLE

America asks that you take immediate heed of what we say in this leaflet.

We are in possession of the most destructive weapon ever designed by man. A single one of our atomic bombs equals the explosive power carried by 2,000 of our Super-Fortresses. This is an awful fact for you to ponder and we solemnly assure you that it is grimly accurate.

We have just begun to use this weapon against your homeland. If you still have any doubt, make inquiry as to what happened to Hiroshima when just one atomic bomb fell on that city.

Before using this bomb again and again to destroy every resource that your military leaders have to prolong this useless war, we ask that you now petition your Emperor to end the war. Our President has outlined for you the thirteen consequences of an honourable surrender. We urge that you accept these consequences and begin the work of building a new, better, and peace-loving Japan.

You should take steps now to cease military resistance. Otherwise, we shall resolutely employ this bomb and all our other superior weapons resolutely and forcefully.

The secretary of the Japanese Cabinet, Sakomiza, felt that:

if the announcement were true, no country could carry on a war. Without the atomic bomb it would be impossible for any country to defend itself against a nation which had the weapon. The chance had come to end the war. It was not necessary to blame the military side, the manufacturing people, or anyone else – just the atomic bomb. It was a good excuse.

But still the military prevaricated. As they did so, the 509th Composite Group prepared to launch the next mission. For the plutonium bomb, the lead aircraft was to be *Bock's*

Car, flown by Major Sweeney, whilst Captain Fred Bock
– who had named the strike plane – would be flying
Sweeney's *Great Artiste* which remained fitted out to drop
the instrumentation after the Hiroshima mission. Shortly
before they took off, the flight engineer on Sweeney's plane
discovered that, as the result of a fuel pump malfunction,
they would not be able to use the reserve fuel tank. After a
hurried conference between Sweeney, Tibbets, Farrell and
Ashworth, it was decided to go ahead anyway – Sweeney
reasoned that they could land on Okinawa or Iwo Jima if
necessary.

Shortly before the final mission, three of the scientists
who had accompanied the plutonium bomb (known as
'Fat Man' because of the bulbous shape of the casing
housing the spherical implosion charges) had received
permission to send their own personal letter with the
instrumentation capsules in the hope of getting a message
to a Japanese physicist who could explain the principles
of the bomb to his government. Philip Morrison, Robert
Serber and Luis Alvarez had studied with Professor
Ryukochi Sagane at the University of California in 1938;
they attached a handwritten letter to each of the three
pods, which read:

> Headquarters
> Atomic Bomb Command
> August 9th 1945

To: Prof R. Sagane
From: Three of your former scientific colleagues during your
stay in the United States.

We are sending this as a personal message to urge that
you use your influence as a reputable nuclear physicist
to convince the Japanese General Staff of the terrible

consequences which will be suffered by your people if you continue in this war.

You have known for several years that an atomic bomb could be built if a nation were willing to pay the enormous cost of preparing the necessary material. Now that you have seen that we have constructed the production plants, there can be no doubt in your mind that all the output of these factories, working 24 hours a day, will be exploded on your homeland.

Within the space of three weeks, we have proof fired one bomb in the American desert, exploded one in Hiroshima, and fired the third one this morning.

We implore you to confirm these facts to your leaders, and to do your utmost to stop the destruction and waste of life which can only result in the total annihilation of all your cities if continued. As scientists, we deplore the use to which a beautiful discovery has been put, but we can assure you that unless Japan surrenders at once, this rain of atomic bombs will increase manyfold in fury.

Bock's Car left Tinian at 1.56 a.m. Japanese time on 9 August, closely followed by the instrument and camera aircraft. Because it was not possible to arm the plutonium bomb in flight there was no reason for the plane to stay low, and it began its slow ascent up to bombing height almost immediately. At 7.45 a.m. the strike aircraft reached the rendezvous point, and began circling, waiting for its two companions. It was here that the first problem with the 'Fat Man' mission appeared: although *the Great Artiste* quickly formed up on the circling strike ship, the camera plane flown by Major Jim Hopkins did not appear –a minor error meant that it was at a different altitude. This was a worry for Sweeney because it meant that both the cameras and the official British observers, Dr

William Penney and Group Captain Leonard Cheshire VC, would miss the explosion. After a tense forty-minute wait, Sweeney decided to continue to Kokura to drop the bomb without Hopkins.

It was at Kokura that the second problem emerged. Although the city had been reported free of cloud, when *Bock's Car* arrived both ground haze and smoke from a nearby fire were obscuring the designated target area. The bombardier Kermit Beahan's orders were strict: he could only bomb visually. On the first pass over Kokura, Beahan ordered 'no drop' and Sweeney took the aircraft round again; on the second pass the same thing happened. By now the flight engineer knew that the aircraft did not have enough fuel left to get it to Iwo Jima, and Beser, the radar countermeasures officer (who was the only man to fly in the strike ship on both atomic missions), was detecting Japanese fighter aircraft activity. As *Bock's Car* circled above Kokura, heavy flak began to range on to it; Sweeney quickly pondered his options. He decided to go for the secondary target: Kokura was spared. Navigator James van Pelt calculated the quickest route to make a bomb run over the secondary target Nagasaki.

As *Bock's Car* approached Nagasaki, the fuel situation was becoming desperate. Kuharek, the flight engineer, had calculated that there was only enough fuel for a single pass over Nagasaki if they were to have any chance of reaching Okinawa, but they could now see that the two-tenth's cloud cover reported by the weather plane four hours before had turned to an almost blanket undercast. Sweeney and Ashworth decided that, if necessary, they would drop the Fat Man by radar, but Ashworth was deeply unhappy at the prospect. They were thirty seconds from the proposed drop point when Beahan spotted a hole in the cloud layer and took control of the plane for a visual drop on a known landmark

1.5 miles from the intended aiming point. In *the Great Artiste* was a *New York Times* correspondent, Bill Laurence, who had been uniquely selected to record this moment:

It was 12.01 and the goal of our mission had arrived. We heard the pre-arranged signal on our radio, put on our arc-welders glasses, and watched tensely the manoeuvrings of the strike ship about half a mile in front of us.

'There she goes!' someone said. Out of the belly of [*Bock's Car*]* what looked like a black object went downward. Our plane swung around to get out of range: but even though we were turning away in the opposite direction, and in spite of the fact that it was broad daylight in our cabin, all of us became aware of a giant flash that broke through the barrier of our arc-welders lenses and flooded our cabin with intense light. We removed our glasses after the first flash, but the light still lingered on, a bluish green light that illuminated the entire sky all around. A tremendous blast wave struck our ship and made it tremble from nose to tail. This was followed by four more blasts in rapid succession, each resounding like the boom of cannon fire, hitting our plane from all directions.

Observers in the tail of our ship saw a giant ball of fire rise as though from the bowels of the earth, belching forth enormous smoke rings. Next they saw a giant pillar of purple fire 10,000 feet high, shooting skyward with enormous speed. By the time our ship had made another turn in the direction of the atomic explosion the pillar of purple fire had reached the level of our altitude. Only about 45 seconds had passed. Awe-struck we watched the pillar of fire shoot upward like

* Laurence actually wrote that *the Great Artiste* dropped the Fat Man. This was probably for security reasons as the aircraft name did not reveal the name of the pilot.

a meteor coming from the earth instead of from outer space, becoming ever more alive as it climbed skyward through the white clouds. It was no longer smoke or dust or even a cloud of fire, it was a living thing, a new species of being, born right before our incredulous eyes. At one stage of its evolution, covering millions of years in terms of seconds, the entity assumed the form of a giant totem pole which at its base was about 3 miles long, tapering off to a mile at the top. Its bottom was brown, its centre amber, its top white. But it was a living totem pole, carved with many grotesque masks grimacing at the earth.

Then, just when it appeared as though the whole thing had settled down into a state of permanence, there came shooting out of the top a giant mushroom that increased the height of the pillar to 45,000 feet. The mushroom top was even more alive than the pillar, seething and boiling in a white fury of creamy foam, sizzling upwards and then descending earthwards, a thousand 'old Faithful' geysers rolled into one.

It kept struggling on in an elemental fury like a creature in the act of breaking the bonds that held it down. In a few seconds it had freed itself from its gigantic stem and floated upwards with a tremendous speed, its momentum carrying it into the stratosphere to a height of 60,000 feet. But no sooner did this happen than another mushroom smaller in size than the first one began emerging out of the pillar. It was as though a decapitated monster was growing a new head.

As the first mushroom floated off into the blue it changed its shape into a flowerlike form, its giant petal curving downward, creamy white outside, rose-coloured inside. It still retained that shape when we last gazed at it from a distance of about 200 miles.

The Fat Man exploded above the Urakami valley district

of Nagasaki. Protected by ground features, 'only' 45,000 or so people were killed or mortally wounded by the blast. The descriptions of the survivors remain as shocking and horrifying as those of Hiroshima. The bomb had had the same effects on those directly exposed to it: the thermal flash – if it had not vaporized or burned its victims to death instantly – raised huge immediate burn blisters over all exposed flesh; the blisters and loosened skin were then blown off by the blast wave. Again, many of the victims died as the result of being smashed by flying debris and by being trapped in collapsed houses that then burned. Many of those without obvious serious injury were inundated with neutrons and gamma radiation, their ability to fight off disease and infection wiped away at a stroke as their bone marrow died. Amongst those caught in the explosion were several hundred Allied prisoners of war, being used as forced labour in the naval dockyard. One, Ron Bryer from North Yorkshire, was sitting in a trench as the Fat Man detonated. He was knocked unconscious but not seriously wounded:

the first real emotion, the first thing I can remember, now slowly coming into my mind, was shame. I started to feel guilty. I looked at my clean hands and I felt ashamed. I got up and decided I'd better get back down there and try to help somebody. Bear in mind, we'd never heard of anything called 'radiation'. We'd never heard of Hiroshima. We just thought that this is one tremendous bloody thing and we'd better get it sorted out.

I found this young Dutch lad, prisoner, lying on the ground, alive. His face was a white sheet – almost pure white as though it had been bleached. It didn't look like any kind of burn to me. I don't know what it looked like. I collected him, helped him up. He could walk. He didn't say anything. At nightfall I found a patch of wet bamboo and I lay down with him all night. I could tell his face was going. The only thing I could find to help him was a little pile of oily rags, just to try to smooth his face. But his ears grew into strange shapes. And the burns on his face developed like water bags. Big, awful things.

Also in Nagasaki were twenty-one refugees from Hiroshima, men and women who had been visiting the first atomic target and who had managed, through great efforts, to get home. Ship designer Tsutomu Yamaguchi was telling his sceptical co-workers about the disaster that had befallen Hiroshima:

'It is beyond common sense!' [my superior] said, 'You are an engineer – calculate it! How could one bomb turn out such huge energy as to destroy a whole city? You were injured, Mr Yamaguchi, your brain was not working.'
    As he was talking, there came the flash. I jumped under the desk immediately, and my superior followed.

Yamaguchi and his superior were uninjured by the Fat Man. Kenshi Hirata, an accountant, had managed to get back to his parents' house in Nagasaki carrying a box in which were the carbonized bones of his young wife, killed at Hiroshima:

while on the way to my wife's home with her bones under my arm, that golden coloured ray whose memory was so vivid in my brains flashed in front of my eyes for the second time. I shouted to my aged father at the top of my voice: 'This is the very flash!' Unconsciously, I shouted again to him: 'Lie face downward!'

In fact, only one of the double victims died: Dr Tsuneo of the Nagasaki Medical College.

The second catastrophic event to strike the Japanese Empire on 9 August was announced by the Soviet Information Bureau:

> In the Far East, Soviet troops have crossed the Manchurian border on a broad front at dawn on 9 August. One Soviet Army, attacking from the Maritime Province, overcame strong initial resistance from the Japanese Kwantung Army, pierced powerful concrete fortifications, crossed the Amur and Ussuri rivers in the Khabarovsk area, and advanced over 9 miles into Manchuria, capturing the town of Fuyuan and other inhabited localities. About 1,000 miles to the west, another Soviet Army, striking south and SE from Transbaikalia, obtained similar initial success.

Only thirteen hours after the detonation of the Fat Man over Nagasaki, the Japanese Supreme War Council sat waiting in an air-raid bunker in Tokyo for their emperor, Hirohito. Although the emperor of Japan had no formal role in the government that was conducted in his name, his power could be said to transcend that of the politicians and soldiers. Within the Shinto religion he was regarded as a descendant of the sun goddess Amaterasu and, though his subjects were under no particular obligation to obey him, it was unthinkable that they would not. Hirohito was present at the meeting as the result of an earlier secret conversation with his prime minister, Kantaro Suzuki, in which he had heard that the only way to break the deadlock between the 'peace' and 'war' factions in the cabinet and the war council was by his own intervention. Suzuki knew that the only way out of the war was now to accept the Potsdam Declaration, provided that some way could be found to preserve the sovereignty of the emperor, but the military – particularly the army – argued that by fighting

yet more desperate and costly battles they could wring
better terms from the Allies. Two meetings of the war
council and cabinet in the afternoon after the Nagasaki
bombing remained deadlocked; in the early hours of the
morning of 10 August, in front of the emperor, the same
situation prevailed.

The split in the Supreme War Council was 3–3 between
the prime minister, foreign minister and navy minister in
favour of peace, and the army minister and the chiefs of staff
of the army and navy in favour of continuing the war. As the
meeting appeared to reach a stalemate in front of Hirohito,
Suzuki dropped his own atomic bomb on the opposition: as
he had secretly agreed with the emperor earlier, he asked
him to advise the meeting. Hirohito spoke:

> I agree with the Foreign Minister's plan. I have given serious
> thought to the situation prevailing at home and abroad and
> have concluded that continuing the war can only mean
> destruction for the nation and a prolongation of bloodshed
> and cruelty in the world. Those who argue for continuing
> the war once assured me that new battalions and supplies
> would be ready at Kujikurihama by June. I realise now that
> this cannot be fulfilled even by September. As for those who
> wish for one last battle here on our own soil, let me remind
> them of the disparity between their previous plans and what
> has actually taken place. I cannot bear to see my innocent
> people struggle any longer. Ending the war is the only way
> to restore world peace and to relieve the nation from the
> terrible distress with which it is burdened.
>
> I cannot help feeling sad when I think of the people who
> have served me so faithfully, the soldiers and sailors who
> have been killed or wounded in far off battles, the families
> who have lost all their worldly goods, and often their lives
> as well, in the air raids at home. It goes without saying that it

is unbearable for me to see the brave and loyal fighting men of Japan disarmed. It is equally unbearable that others who have rendered me devoted service should now be punished as instigators of war. Nevertheless, the time has come when we must bear the unbearable.

When I think of the feelings of my Imperial Grandfather, Emperor Meiji, at the time of the Triple Intervention, I cannot but swallow my tears and sanction the proposal to accept the Allied proclamation on the basis outlined by the Foreign Minister.

Amazed, the Supreme War Council accepted their Emperor's advice. Immediately after leaving the Palace, the cabinet met to draft a reply accepting the terms of the Potsdam Declaration 'with the understanding that the said declaration does not comprise any demand which prejudices the prerogatives of His Majesty as Sovereign ruler'.

The Japanese acceptance of the Potsdam Declaration reached Washington on the morning of 10 August, local time. At a meeting at the White House, Truman, Byrnes (who was now Secretary of State), Stimson, Forrestal (Secretary of the Navy) and Admiral William Leahy, the White House Chief of Staff, agreed that Japan's offer was acceptable in principle, but their reply stressed that:

The ultimate form of government shall, in accordance with the Potsdam Declaration, be established by the freely expressed will of the Japanese people.

Later the same day, Truman ordered that the atomic bombing of Japan be suspended. Groves had been preparing to organize the transportation of the second plutonium core to Tinian ready for use on or after the 17th or 18th of August; the target had not been fixed but would quite likely have been Tokyo – or what remained of it – to show the Japanese government precisely what they were facing. Many were relieved by this decision. Truman himself had told his cabinet that:

> the thought of wiping out another 100,000 people was too horrible. He didn't like the idea of killing, as he said, 'all those kids'.

Washington's ambiguous reply to Japan's message of acceptance allowed the 'hawks' in Tokyo one last avenue to resist surrender: they argued that they could not countenance surrender without a guarantee that the emperor would not be dethroned. Fierce debate continued for three days as elements in the military sought support for a *coup d'état* against the Suzuki government, but again it was the emperor who brought matters to a head.

Guided by Prime Minister Suzuki and members of his household, the emperor summoned a meeting of the Supreme War Council and cabinet on 14 August at the Imperial Palace. Choked by emotion, he reiterated his decision that Japan surrender to the Allies; his decision brooked no argument: the war was over. At noon on 15 August, Hirohito spoke over the radio to his people for the first time:

> To our good and loyal subjects. After pondering deeply the general trends of the world, and the actual conditions obtaining in our Empire today, we have decided to effect a settlement of the present situation by resorting to an extraordinary measure. We have ordered our Government to communicate to the Governments of the United States, Great Britain, China and the Soviet Union that our Empire accepts the provisions of their joint declaration.

To strive for the common prosperity and happiness of all nations as well as the security and well being of our subjects is the solemn obligation which has been handed down by our Imperial Ancestors, and which we lay close to our heart. Indeed, we declared war on America and Britain out of our sincere desire to ensure Japan's self-preservation and the stabilisation of Southeast Asia, it being far from our thought either to infringe upon the sovereignty of other nations or to embark upon territorial aggrandisement.

But now the war has lasted nearly four years. Despite the best that has been done by everyone – the gallant fighting of military and naval forces, the diligence and assiduity of our servants of the State, and the devoted service of our one hundred million people – the war situation has developed not necessarily to Japan's advantage, while the general trends of the world have all turned against her interest.

Moreover, the enemy has begun to employ a new and most cruel bomb, the power of which to do damage is indeed incalculable, taking the toll of many innocent lives. Should we continue to fight, it would not only result in an ultimate collapse and obliteration of the Japanese nation, but would also lead to the total extinction of human civilisation. Such being the case, how are we to save the millions of our subjects, or to atone ourselves before the hallowed spirits of our Imperial Ancestors? This is the reason why we have ordered the acceptance of the provisions of the joint declaration of the Powers.

To the utter astonishment of many of Japan's population of 100 million, a significant minority of whom assumed that the war was rumoured to be coming to an end because Japan had *won*, Emperor Hirohito led his nation into surrender just eight days after the destruction of Hiroshima.

7

Epilogue

No nuclear weapon has been used operationally since the Fat Man fell on Nagasaki on 9 August 1945. Since that day, those in possession of nuclear weapons have managed to resist the temptation to employ them – although this has supposedly been a close call in some situations. Shortly after the war had come to an end, though before the official surrender ceremonies, a Japanese news agancy reported that:

Nagasaki is now a dead city, all areas have been literally razed to the ground. Only a few buildings are left, standing conspicuously amongst the ashes.

The aftermath of the Nagasaki bombing gave many of those who had been involved in the decision to use the terrible new weapons a chance to reflect. Henry Stimson, the United State Secretary of War, had always been troubled by the enormity of using weapons of mass destruction:

I see too many stern and heart rending decisions to be

willing to pretend that war is anything other than what it is. The face of war is the face of death; death is an inevitable part of every order that a wartime leader gives. The decision to use the atomic bomb was a decision that brought death to over a hundred thousand Japanese. No explanation can change that and I do not wish to gloss it over.

But this deliberate, premeditated destruction was our least abhorrent alternative. The destruction of Hiroshima and Nagasaki put an end to the Japanese war. It stopped the fire raids, and the strangling blockade; it ended the ghastly spectre of a clash of great land armies.

In this last great action of the Second World War we were given the final proof that war is death.

Winston Churchill's view was that:

To avert a vast, indefinite butchery, to bring the war to an end, to give peace to the world, to lay healing hands upon its tortured peoples by a manifestation of overwhelming power at the cost of a few explosions, seemed, after all our toils and perils, a miracle of deliverance.

For them, there was little doubt that the bomb had to be used and no guilt at the role that they had played in its evolution. Others disagreed. Admiral Leahy felt:

The use of this barbarous weapon at Hiroshima and Nagasaki was of no material assistance in our war against Japan. The Japanese were already defeated and ready to surrender because of the effective sea blockade and the successful bombing with conventional weapons . . .

My own feeling was that in being the first to use it, we had adopted an ethical standard common to the barbarians of the dark ages. I was not taught to make war in that fashion and

wars cannot be won by destroying women and children . . .
One of the professors associated with the Manhattan Project
told me that he had hoped the bomb wouldn't work. I wish
that he had been right.

His doubts were shared by others who had been closer to
the project. Otto Frisch felt that:

there was the argument that this slaughter had saved
the lives of many more Americans *and* Japanese who would
have died in the slow process of conquest by which the war
might have had to be ended had there been no atom bomb.
But few of us could see any moral reason for dropping a
second bomb (on Nagasaki) only a few days later, even
though that brought the war to an immediate halt. Most
of us thought that the Japanese would have surrendered
within a few days anyhow. But this is a subject that has
been endlessly debated and never settled.

The argument over whether use of the atomic bomb actually saved lives remains unresolved; indeed, it is unlikely
ever to be settled to the satisfaction of all sides; but it is
worth examining other factors which may have influenced
the decision to drop the bomb. It should be remembered that
one of the most important factors which helped persuade
the governments of the United States and Great Britain to
authorize vast sums of money to be spent developing the
bomb was the fear that Germany, under the deeply unstable,
vicious and unpredictable rule of Adolf Hitler's Nazi Party,
might get there first and use it decisively in its war of expansion in Europe. Indeed, in possession of nuclear weapons,
the monumental folly of Hitler's unprovoked declaration of
war on the United States in the wake of Pearl Harbor would
not seem quite so crazy.

But Germany did not develop an atomic bomb and it was not seriously making the attempt to do so. The war in Europe came to an end three months before an operational atomic bomb could be made ready for use and, in any case, the Germans' ability to resist was effectively ended some months before that. The collapse of Germany, however, left the Manhattan Project with several problems, both ethical and practical.

When the war in Europe ended in May 1945, the war against Japan was expected to continue well into 1946 and it was assumed that Allied casualties would continue to mount. Even so, it was clear to Allied intelligence personnel that Japan was at the end of its resources and had, in fact, been sliding steadily towards defeat since the Battle of Midway, just seven months after Pearl Harbor; crippled by poor strategic thinking and a lack of raw materials, Japan's decision to resort to war had been foolish in the extreme. At the same time, Japan's nuclear research programme was limited even in comparison to the German effort: the sacrifices involved in keeping the conventional Japanese war machine running ruled out anything more than low-level theoretical research, and it would have been inconceivable for the Japanese to have built industrial plant on the same scale as for the Manhattan Project. In short, just as the fear of German atomic weapons had proved a chimera, there was no threat of Japanese nuclear bombardment of Allied targets.

The fact is that the simple, historically valid, reason that the bombs were dropped was the hope that they would shock the intractably divided Japanese government into decisive action to end the war. The truth is that they did. But there can be no doubt that it was a deeply bitter shock for the people of Hiroshima and Nagasaki to absorb.

On 5 March 1947, Sir Winston Churchill told an audience

at Westminster College, Fulton, Missouri, that 'An iron curtain has descended across the continent.' The end of World War II had brought peace to Europe, but it was a watchful peace between two great power blocs. In the west, the democracies under the leadership of the United States were faced off against the eastern 'Communist' countries inspired by Stalin's Soviet Union.

For many people, peace in 1945 merely meant swopping one form of miserable totalitarian rule – that of the Nazis – for the equally nasty rule of Soviet-controlled puppets. A crucial factor that prevented the Soviets from attempting to extend their rule forcibly into the remainder of Europe was the possession by the United States of nuclear weaponry. But in the face of this enormous US advantage, an arms race developed that was to persist until the beginning of this decade and which was ultimately to destroy the Soviet form of Communism.

The Cold War, as it quickly became known, was fought at many levels, from overt confrontations like the Berlin Blockade and the Cuban Missile crisis down to subliminal propaganda smears. Some of the most fiercely fought battles were in the world of intelligence. Klaus Fuchs, a German refugee of Communist inclinations, was recruited to provide information on atomic weaponry even before the end of the war:

> I was asked to help Professor Peierls in Birmingham, on some war work. I accepted it and I started work without knowing what the war work was. I doubt whether it would have made any difference to my subsequent actions if I had known the nature of the work beforehand. When I learned the purpose of the work I decided to inform Russia and I established contact through another member of the Communist Party . . . At this time I had complete

confidence in Russian policy and I believed that the Western Allies deliberately allowed Russia and Germany to fight each other to the death.

Partly as a result of Fuchs' espionage, the Soviet Union exploded its first experimental atomic bomb – Joe 1 – in September 1949. It was from this moment that the Cold War became a nuclear confrontation.

Group Captain Leonard Cheshire VC, one of the two official British witnesses at the bombing of Nagasaki, came to the conclusion that:

> The lesson of Hiroshima and Nagasaki is that the side that has the bomb is unfightable. You cannot fight the bomb and survive as a nation.

But the situation after Joe 1 was changed. Now both sides had the bomb. The obvious answer seemed to be to build more and better bombs in an effort to gain a strategic advantage over the opposition in order to be able to force retreat or concessions, and both the US and the Soviet Union tried to do so; independently producing thermonuclear 'supers', in which an atomic bomb acts as a trigger to start a fusion reaction in deuterium atoms; developing rockets which could not be intercepted; and developing submarines which could not be detected before the unstoppable missiles were launched. No concessions were forthcoming.

Despite the addition of Great Britain, France and China to the group of countries which possess their own atomic weapons, a stalemate persisted from the 1950s to the end of the 1980s between the western countries, united beneath the banner of Nato, and the Soviets and China, divided despite their supposedly similar ideologies, but equally threatening.

The 'threat' that nuclear weapons posed – because of their ability to blast and irradiate out of existence the products of modern civilization – created an intense debate in the democratic countries. On one side were disarmers, a species of absolute pacifist, who claimed that possession of nuclear weapons amounted to a moral outrage, a temptation to politicians and militarists, and served no practical purpose. On the other side stood contingent pacifists, who argued that to give up atomic weapons simply amounted to handing a blackmail tool to anyone that chose to continue to possess them, and who believed that their existence was a guarantee against major war. To one side of this debate stood the military of the major powers, planning scenarios in which they could employ nuclear weapons short of an all-out exchange involving world destruction.

In April 1980, at the height of the debate, Professor E. P. Thompson published an appeal for nuclear disarmament in Europe:

> We are entering the most dangerous decade in human history. A third world war is not merely possible, but increasingly likely. Economic and social difficulties in advanced industrial countries, crisis, militarism and war in the third world compound the political tensions that fuel a demented arms race. In Europe, the main geographical stage for the East–West confrontation, new generations of ever more deadly nuclear weapons are appearing.
>
> For at least twenty-five years, the forces of both the North Atlantic and the Warsaw alliance have each had sufficient nuclear weapons to annihilate their opponents, and at the same time to endanger the very basis of civilised life. But with each passing year, competition in nuclear armaments has multiplied their numbers, increasing the probability of some devastating accident or miscalculation.

As each side tries to prove its readiness to use nuclear weapons, in order to prevent their use by the other side, new, more 'usable' nuclear weapons are designed and the idea of 'limited' nuclear war is made to sound more and more plausible. So much so that this paradoxical process can logically only lead to the actual use of nuclear weapons.

Neither of the major powers is now in any moral position to influence smaller countries to forgo the acquisition of nuclear armament. The increasing spread of nuclear reactors and the growth of the industry that installs them, reinforce the likelihood of world wide proliferation of nuclear weapons, thereby multiplying the risks of nuclear exchanges.

Over the years, public opinion has pressed for nuclear disarmament and detente between the contending military blocs. This pressure has failed. An increasing proportion of world resources is expended on weapons, even though mutual extermination is already amply guaranteed. This economic burden, in both East and West, contributes to growing social and political strain, setting in motion a vicious circle in which the arms race feeds upon the instability of the world economy and vice-versa: a deathly dialectic.

We are now in great danger. Generations have been born beneath the shadow of nuclear war, and have become habituated to the threat. Concern has given way to apathy. Meanwhile, in a world living always under menace, fear extends through both halves of the European continent. The powers of the military and of internal security forces are enlarged, limitations are placed upon free exchanges of ideas and between persons, and civil rights of independent-minded individuals are threatened, in the West as well as the East.

We do not wish to apportion guilt between the political

and military leaders of East and West. Guilt lies squarely upon both parties. Both parties have adopted menacing postures and committed aggressive actions in different parts of the world.

The remedy lies in our own hands. We must act together to free the entire territory of Europe, from Poland to Portugal, from nuclear weapons, air and submarine bases, and from all institutions engaged in research into or manufacture of nuclear weapons. We ask the two superpowers to withdraw all nuclear weapons from European territory. In particular, we ask the Soviet Union to halt production of SS-20 medium-range missiles and we ask the United States not to implement the decision to develop cruise missiles and Pershing II missiles for deployment in Western Europe. We also urge the ratification of the SALT II agreement, as a necessary step towards the renewal of effective negotiations on general and complete disarmament.

At the same time, we must defend and extend the right of all citizens, East or West, to take part in this common movement and to engage in every kind of exchange.

We appeal to our friends in Europe, of every faith and persuasion, to consider urgently the ways in which we can work together for these common objectives. We envisage a European-wide campaign, in which every kind of exchange takes place; in which representatives of different nations and opinions confer and co-ordinate their activities; and in which less formal exchanges, between universities, churches, women's organisations, trade unions, youth organisations, professional groups and individuals, take place with the object of promoting a common object: to free all of Europe from nuclear weapons.

We must commence to act as if a united, neutral and pacific Europe already exists. We must learn to be loyal, not to 'East' or 'West', but to each other, and we must disregard the prohibitions and limitations imposed by any national state.

It will be the responsibilty of the people of each nation to agitate for the expulsion of nuclear weapons and bases from European soil and territorial waters, and to decide upon its own means and strategy, concerning its own territory. These will differ from one country to another, and we do not suggest that any single strategy should be imposed. But this must be part of a trans-continental movement in which every kind of exchange takes place.

We must resist any attempt by the statesmen of East or West to manipulate this movement to their own advantage. We offer no advantage to either Nato or the Warsaw Alliance. Our objectives must be to free Europe from confrontation, to enforce detente between the United States and the Soviet Union, and, ultimately, to dissolve both great power alliances.

In appealing to fellow Europeans, we are not turning our backs on the world. In working for the peace of Europe we are working for the peace of the world. Twice this century Europe has disgraced its claims to civilisation by engendering world war. This time we must repay our debts to the world by engendering peace.

This appeal will achieve nothing if it is not supported by determined and inventive action, to win more people to support it. We need to mount an irresistible pressure for a Europe free of nuclear weapons.

We do not wish to impose any uniformity on the movement nor to pre-empt the consultations and decisions of those many organisations already exercising their influence for disarmament and peace. But the situation is urgent. The dangers steadily advance. We invite your support for this common objective, and we shall welcome both your help and advice.

Two years later, the British prime minister, Margaret Thatcher, summed up the case against nuclear disarmament at the United Nations General Assembly:

> The fundamental risk to peace is not the existence of weapons of particular types. It is the disposition on the part of some states to impose change on others by resorting to force against other nations and not in 'arms races' whether real or imaginary. Aggressors do not start wars because an adversary has built up his own strength. They start wars because they believe they can gain more by going to war than by remaining at peace . . . I do not believe that armaments cause wars [or that] action on them alone will . . . prevent wars. It is not merely a mistaken analysis but an evasion of responsibility to suppose that we can prevent the horrors of war by focussing on its instruments. They are more often symptoms than causes.

Although the Cold War ended with the collapse of Soviet Communism at the beginning of this decade, an event which was itself caused by the effective self-bankrupting of the dire and corrupt Soviet economic system in its attempt to match western military expenditure, nuclear weapons remain a threat, albeit at a reduced level, but there seems no way to get rid of them. A schoolgirl survivor of Hiroshima wrote afterwards:

> Those scientists who invented the atomic bomb, what did they think would happen if they dropped it?

Appendix 1

Biographical Information

Abelson, Philip. A student of Luis Alvarez at Berkeley who subsequently became a key member of the small group that discovered neptunium. His contribution to the Manhattan Project was in the separation of uranium isotopes.

Alvarez, Luis W. Theoretical physicist at Berkeley who invented the detonators used in the plutonium implosion bomb and took part in the Hiroshima mission as a member of the crew of *the Great Artiste*. Together with Philip Morrison and Robert Serber he attached messages to the measuring instruments dropped with the Fat Man bomb at Nagasaki, addressed to a Japanese nuclear physicist, calling on him to explain the irresistible power of the bomb to his government.

Anderson, Herbert L. Assisted Fermi in building the first working reactor in Chicago and devised fall-out experiments for use at the Alamogordo (Trinity) test.

Bainbridge, Kenneth. American physicist who had worked with Rutherford in England and attended several meetings of the British MAUD Committee in 1941, where he became convinced that a uranium bomb was possible. Was involved in the development of the implosion bomb and given responsibility for organizing the Trinity test. Bainbridge subsequently became the professor of physics at Harvard.

Beahan, Kermit. Bombardier aboard *Bock's Car*, which dropped the Fat Man bomb on Nagasaki. Beahan was known in the air force as 'the Great Artiste', hence the name of his usual aircraft (*the Great Artiste's* crew flew in *Bock's Car* for the Nagasaki mission). His offer to visit Nagasaki and apologize for the damage in 1985 was not accepted by the people of Nagasaki.

Bethe, Hans. German physicist working under Hans Geiger at Tübingen University, who was dismissed in 1933 for being Jewish. Thereafter settled in the US in 1935 as an associate professor at Cornell. Bethe was named head of the theoretical division at Los Alamos and played a major role in the development of both operational bombs, as well as sitting on the Target Committee. One of Bethe's greatest achievements was his explanation of the nuclear fusion process that fuels the stars.

Bohr, Niels. Danish theoretical physicist of enormous international standing and importance. Having studied under Rutherford in the early years of the twentieth century, he made great contributions to the understanding of atomic structure, including the liquid drop' model of the structure of the nucleus. He was smuggled out of German-occupied Denmark in October 1943 with his family to join the 'British' contingent at Los Alamos. By the time the bomb had become reality, Bohr was extremely concerned by its implications for international security, and lobbied both Churchill and Roosevelt in an effort to persuade them to share nuclear secrets with the Soviets and so reduce international paranoia and prevent an arms race. It has since been suggested that he was an unwitting intelligence source for the Soviet secret service, although he had little or no sympathy for any form of authoritarian government.

Bothe, Walther. Although a brilliant scientist and eventual Nobel prize winner, Bothe is also remembered for his mistakes. In 1930 he conducted experiments bombarding materials with alpha radiation; he found that these gave off a powerful emission which he incorrectly identified as gamma rays – in fact they were neutrons, as Chadwick later ascertained. In 1940 he incorrectly measured the neutron absorption cross-section of carbon, leading German scientists to conclude that they would have to use heavy water to construct their reactors and crippling the German nuclear research effort.

Bush, Vannevar. An electrical engineer by training, Bush was the dean of the school of engineering at the Massachusetts Institute of Technology and then the president of the Carnegie Institute before being nominated by President Roosevelt as head of the National Defense Research Council in the summer of 1940 with responsibility for funding basic uranium research. Bush subsequently successfully lobbied for the setting up of an Office of Scientific Research and Development, of which he became the first director in 1941. As director of the OSRD, he was the effective civilian head of the atomic bomb project. Although Bush was not a nuclear physicist, he was sufficiently far-sighted to recognize the potential of nuclear weapons and can be credited with mobilizing the successful US effort.

Chadwick, James. A former student of Rutherford who proved the existence of the neutron in 1932. Chadwick became professor of physics at Liverpool University and there worked with Otto Frisch and Joseph Rotblat on fission research between 1940 and 1943. During this period he was a member of the MAUD Committee which persuaded the British (and US) government that nuclear weapons were possible. At Los Alamos he was the 'leader' of the British scientists.

Conant, James B. The president of Harvard University, he was a close associate of Vannevar Bush and succeeded him as chairman of the NDRC. Acted as one of the senior civilian leaders of the atomic bomb project from 1942.

Einstein, Albert. One of the two or three most important theoreticians since Newton, Einstein developed the special and general theories of relativity which, amongst other things, pointed out the equivalence of mass and energy in the famous equation $E = mc^2$. Einstein was also active politically, strongly opposing the rise of Nazism in Germany in the 1920s and 1930s. In 1939, Einstein was approached by Leo Szilard, Eugene Wigner, Edward Teller and Enrico Fermi to write to President Roosevelt alerting him to the possibilities of nuclear fission in bomb making. Einstein played no active part in the bomb project but remained a sounding-board for some of the senior scientists. Although Einstein's grandfatherly countenance has become the paradigm of the appearance of the cultured intellectual, he remained into old age a strongly built and very heavily muscled man.

Fermi, Enrico. Fermi's attempts during the 1930s to create transuranic elements by bombarding uranium with neutrons led, indirectly, to the discovery of nuclear fission by Otto Hahn. Fermi himself was based in Rome until 1938 but fled to the US after receiving the Nobel prize to protect his Jewish wife from persecution by the Fascists. Fermi was one of the first to realize the dangers inherent in nuclear fission and became part of the group that prevailed on Einstein to write to President Roosevelt in 1939. Subsequently, his experimentation led him to construct and operate the world's first nuclear reactor in 1942. Working at Los Alamos together with Edward Teller he worked out the requirements necessary for a thermonuclear ('hydrogen') bomb.

Ferebee, Major Thomas. Highly experienced US air force bombardier who was selected as Group Bombardier for the 509th. Flew the Hiroshima mission as bombardier on *Enola Gay* and was responsible for releasing the bomb, which exploded just a few hundred feet from its notional aiming point.

Frisch, Otto R. An Austrian-born physicist of Jewish descent, Frisch played an understated but crucial part in the development of the atomic bomb at several stages. Nazi racial laws forced him to leave Germany in 1933 and he went to work in Britain and in Denmark with Bohr. Whilst spending Christmas with his aunt Lise Meitner in Sweden in 1938 they together interpreted some results of Otto Hahn's neutron bombardment experiments to show that nuclear fission had taken place. He was working in England during the early part of the war and there, with another refugee from Nazi Germany, Rudolph Peierls, calculated the size of the critical mass of pure uranium 235, proving that it would be no more than a few kilograms. Frisch and Peierls' calculations convinced the British, and subsequently the American, scientific and political establishments that an atomic bomb was feasible. Frisch went to Los Alamos as part of the British team in 1943 and there performed the 'Dragon' series of experiments to calculate the precise size of the critical masses for the uranium and plutonium bombs.

He ended his career as professor of physics and director of the Cavendish Laboratory at Cambridge University.

Groves, General Leslie R. West Point graduate US army engineer selected as military commander of the 'Manhattan Engineer District' and thus placed in effective overall control of the project. Although Groves has subsequently been criticized as a virtual egomaniac who wilfully ignored directives and orders that he did not agree with, the fact remains that he steered the project with great skill and tenacity and achieved his aim: the construction of operational nuclear weapons. Groves was never popular with his subordinates but he did have a knack for selecting the right people for the job, including Oppenheimer as his scientific director. Groves attempted to circumvent US government policy, which admitted the British as full partners in the programme, and was largely successful in keeping British representatives away from the operational aspects of the attacks on Hiroshima and Nagasaki, although he had to allow British observers to see the Nagasaki bomb. He was subsequently able to help persuade President Truman and his secretary of state, Byrnes, to exclude Britain from nuclear technology.

Goudsmit, Samuel. Physics professor at the University of Michigan of Dutch-Jewish background, Goudsmit was appointed scientific director of ALSOS, the mission to track down Nazi nuclear scientists and their materials. A pre-war friend of Heisenberg and several other senior German scientists, he ascertained that the German research was far behind Allied efforts in what he characterized as a 'race' for the bomb.

Hahn, Otto. A German chemist, Hahn virtually invented the science of 'radiochemistry'. He worked closely with his friend and colleague Lise Meitner for thirty years until she was forced to leave Germany as a Jewish refugee. Thereafter he continued to correspond with her and, in December 1938, sent her a letter detailing the strange results of an experiment to bombard uranium atoms with neutrons. Hahn had ascertained that the actual products of these experiments were barium and lanthanum rather than the transuranic elements that other physicists claimed to have found. Meitner and her nephew Otto Frisch realized that fission had taken place.

Heisenberg, Werner. German physicist who made important contributions to the understanding of the nucleus and to quantum theory (Heisenberg's uncertainty principle). During the war he was put in charge of uranium research at the Kaiser Wilhelm Institute in Berlin and became convinced that Germany would not be able to develop an atomic bomb during the conflict; instead he directed his efforts to building a heavy-water moderated reactor, a project that failed.

Kistiakowsky, George. Ukrainian born chemist who became professor at Harvard in 1938. Kistiakowsky was responsible for producing the explosive charges that would create a spherical detonation wave to implode the plutonium core of the Fat Man bombs.

Lawrence, Ernest O. Professor of physics at Berkeley, Lawrence invented the cyclotron particle accelerator which produced the first recognized samples of plutonium. A senior figure in pushing for a US bomb programme, his contribution to the Manhattan Project was in the separation of uranium isotopes.

McMillan, Edwin. Chemist at Berkeley who, with Abelson, created the first transuranic element, neptunium. Worked at Los Alamos as a radiochemist and on the problems of implosion and gun-type bombs.

Meitner, Lise. Austrian-Jewish chemist who worked for many years in Berlin with Otto Hahn, where they jointly discovered element 91, protactinium. Forced to leave Germany in 1938 because of Nazi persecution, she went to live in Sweden where, with her nephew Otto Frisch, she correctly deduced the process of nuclear fission.

Oliphant, Mark. An Australian physicist who became professor at Birmingham University in England. Became a member of the MAUD Committee, which supervised early British nuclear research, and helped to galvanize the US scientific community into action during a visit to the US in 1941. Worked on isotope separation for the Manhattan Project and subsequently became the governor of South Australia.

Oppenheimer, Robert. US-born nuclear physicist of German-Jewish descent. After an education at Harvard and various European universities, Oppenheimer became professor of physics at Berkeley studying various nuclear and cosmological phenomena and predicting, amongst other things, the existence of 'Black Holes' in space. In 1943 he was nominated as the scientific director of the Los Alamos laboratory and thus of the bomb project; thereafter, he worked closely with General Groves, assembling a team of enormous talent and intellect, to steer through the production of the bomb. Although a scientific genius, he was politically naive and had, during the 1930s, associated himself with various left-wing causes and individuals. This led, in 1954, to his being denounced as a crypto-Communist by McCarthyite witch-hunters and losing his security clearance and job at the US Atomic Energy Commission; in part, this was the result of his objection to the development of the thermonuclear hydrogen bomb.

Peierls, Rudolf. A German-Jewish refugee who escaped from Nazism to work at Birmingham University in England. There, in 1940, he calculated with Frisch that the critical mass of uranium required to build a bomb was small enough to make a weapon practical. Subsequently he was involved in developing the gaseous diffusion method of isotope separation and with the problems of creating a practical 'weaponized' bomb.

Penney, William G. British theoretical physicist who was co-opted onto the Target Committee for the operational bombings and then flew in the Nagasaki bombing with Group Captain Cheshire as an official British observer. When the US reneged on wartime agreements to share nuclear weapons technology with Britain, Penney led the British team which designed and built British nuclear and thermonuclear bombs.

Rutherford, Ernest. New-Zealand-born physicist who became the great figure of atomic discovery through his forty-year career. Apart from his discovery of various subatomic particles and his explanation of the planetary structure of the atom, he was also responsible for teaching many of the other great physicists who followed him, including Bohr. Died after a minor accident in 1937.

Seaborg, Glenn T. Chemist at Berkeley who worked with McMillan on neptunium research and then discovered plutonium after McMillan had left to work on radar projects. Thereafter led the research effort that proved the fissibility of plutonium and devised the processes for extracting it from irradiated uranium that led to its use in the Fat Man and subsequent atomic weapons.

Simon, Franz. Jewish refugee from Nazi Germany who worked at Oxford University. There he led the team that devised the process for separating U235 by gaseous diffusion.

Sweeney, Major Charles. US air force pilot who flew *Bock's Car* to Nagasaki for the Fat Man mission. Dogged by a series of problems, Sweeney showed enormous skill in getting to his target and getting back again when very low on fuel.

Szilard, Leo. Born in Hungary, Szilard led a nomadic life around Europe and the US in the years leading up to World War II. Whilst strolling through London in 1934, he had the notion that it might be possible to start a chain reaction in certain atoms in which an enormous release of energy might take place. He worked his ideas out and patented them, assigning the rights to the British admiralty. In subsequent years he began to come to the conclusion that he was probably wrong and had just written to the admiralty to tell them that there was no need to maintain the patent when he heard about Frisch and Meitner's fission hypothesis. Szilard immediately realized the significance of this and began a campaign to alert the US government to the prospects of nuclear weapons, which resulted in the letter sent by his friend Albert Einstein in 1939; at the same time, he tried to persuade scientists in the US to keep the results of fission experiments secret to prevent Nazi Germany from advancing in bomb technology. In the early war years he worked closely with Fermi and was present when Fermi's reactor went critical in Chicago in 1942. As the end of the war in Europe approached and it became obvious that Nazi Germany had not developed nuclear weapons, Szilard began quietly campaigning for the bomb not to be used against Japan. As a result, he came to be regarded as a nuisance and was excluded from the inner circles of bomb research.

Teller, Edward. A Jewish Hungarian who left Berlin to avoid Nazi persecution, Teller worked in the US where he was, in the 1930s, a close associate of Leo Szilard. Teller was closely involved in the Einstein letter to Roosevelt and, with Fermi in 1942, worked out how a thermonuclear bomb might work. At Los Alamos, Teller was assigned by Oppenheimer to the theoretical division, where he continued to work on the 'super' (hydrogen) bomb. This work culminated in the 1950s with the successful hydrogen bomb design that is still in use (and is still secret).

Thomson, George. Professor of physics at Imperial College in London who began experimentation in 1939 with thoughts of a nuclear weapon in mind. Subsequently became chairman of the MAUD Committee, which produced the report that effectively started the Manhattan Project.

Tibbets, Colonel Paul. Highly experienced US air force bomber pilot who was selected to lead and train the 509th Bomber Group for the operational use of atomic bombs. A highly intelligent man, Tibbets had given up medical studies to become a pilot. He personally piloted the B-29 *Enola Gay*, which he had named after his mother, on the Hiroshima raid on 6 August 1945.

Ulam, Stanislaw. A Polish mathematician, Ulam was teaching in the US when Germany's unprovoked attack on Poland cut him off from his homeland. Ulam was invited to go to Los Alamos in the winter of 1943 and was assigned to Teller's group, where he worked on calculations for the 'super' bomb and on implosion calculations. After the war he originated the concept, with Edward Teller, that led to the design of the hydrogen bomb.

Wigner, Eugene. Hungarian-Jewish refugee from Nazi persecution who was a close associate of Leo Szilard and helped persuade Einstein to write to Roosevelt in 1939. Subsequently worked closely with Fermi on reactor designs and directed theoretical research at the Chicago Met-Lab.

Zinn, Walter. American physicist who assisted Fermi in his crucial reactor experiments in Chicago. Thereafter he worked on reactor design, building the first electricity generating reactor, the first submarine power unit and the first breeder reactor.

Appendix 2

Bibliography and Sources

This book is, in effect, an anthology of material culled from both primary and secondary sources and I am very grateful to copyright holders, where applicable, for their permission to publish material still covered by copyright. Every effort has been made to trace copyright holders but I hope that those I have not been able to find will accept my apologies. About 50 per cent of the quotations have been culled from newspaper reporting and features published during the past 50 years, but the remainder were from individuals quoted in the following published works:

Bickel, Lennard	*The Deadly Element*, Macmillan, 1980
British Mission to Japan	*The Effects of the Atomic Bombs at Hiroshima and Nagasaki*, HMSO, 1946
Churchill, Winston	*The Second World War*, Cassell, 1951
Craig, William	*The Fall of Japan*, Weidenfeld and Nicolson, 1968
Dollinger, Hans	*The Decline and Fall of Nazi Germany and Imperial Japan*, Odhams Books, 1968
Frisch, Otto	*What Little I Remember*, Cambridge University Press, 1979

Hahn, Otto   *A Scientific Autobiography*, Charles
                             Scribner's Sons, 1966
Hersey, John   *Hiroshima*, Penguin, 1946
Irving, David   *The Virus House*, William Kimber,
                             1967
Patterson, Walter C.   *The Plutonium Business*, Wildwood
                             House, 1984
Peierls, R. E. and   *Science News 2*, Penguin, 1947
  Enogat, John
Powers, Thomas   *Heisenberg's War*, Jonathan Cape, 1993
Rhodes, Richard   *The Making of the Atomic Bomb*,
                             Penguin, 1988
Snow, C. P.   *The Physicists*, Little Brown, 1981
Thatcher, Margaret   *The Downing Street Years*, Harper
                             Collins, 1993
Thomas, Gordon and   *Ruin from the Air*, Hamish Hamilton,
  Witts, Max Morgan   1977
Thompson, E. P. and   *Protest and Survive*, Penguin, 1980
  Smith, Dan(eds)
Williams, Robert Chadwell   *Klaus Fuchs, Atom Spy*, Harvard, 1987

Appendix 3

The Physics of the Bomb

P. A. Morrison

From *Science News*, issue no. 2, 1946

NUCLEAR ENERGY CONTROLLED: THE PILE. The Hiroshima explosion signalled to the world that the large-scale release of nuclear energy had been achieved. The spectacular and terrible detonation drew all attention to the catastrophic release of energy which in the bomb had been made possible. Even now that the facts of the matter are known, a belief remains that the 'control' of nuclear energy is still beyond our means. Nothing could be further from the truth. The nuclear chain reaction has operated literally every day from December 2, 1942, until now. It has worked in one of the several existing forms of piles, or chain reactors, whether the uncooled pile of graphite blocks and UO_2 lumps which was man's first nuclear reactor, or the huge plutonium-producing units at Hanford which quietly warm the Columbia River. This is operated with a small reproduction factor so that the number of neutrons produced in a generation of the chain by a single neutron reaches unity *only* after the delayed neutron emission from the fission fragments has occurred. By this means the chain reactor is made into a smooth and trouble-free device. Probably no other machine can be made to operate successfully over such a great range of intensity, and stabilized at any operating power level allowed by the engineering design by the simple motion of a single control element. No complicated moving mechanism or delicate vacuum system forms part of a chain reactor. The steadiness and smoothness are noteworthy; the system is inherently stable. And why not, for the only moving parts are neutrons! At both the Argonne and the Clinton piles, one minor problem has been to provide a routine of meter-reading and recording exacting enough to ensure that the man who is operating the pile does not find it too easy to fall asleep. The normal demands of keeping the pile intensity constant are so easily met that the operator has very little to do. Starting and stopping the reactor is simply a matter of displacing the control rods by a predetermined amount.

The problem before the whole Manhattan Project, given the production of quantities of fissionable material, was to make the chain reaction uncontrolled and explosive. The Los Alamos laboratory was given this problem, and its practical solution was in almost every detail conceived and executed there. While the scale of the operations at Los Alamos is far smaller than that at the great production plants, the diversity and the difficulty of the research and production there carried out make the site a unique and incredible one. Military security regulations still prohibit the discussion of many of the interesting problems there solved, but following the Smyth report and making obvious extensions of previous knowledge very much of the physics of the bomb can be discussed.

THE MEANING OF A MICROSECOND. It was clear from the beginning that the great piles of uranium and moderator could not make satisfactory military weapons. In the first place, they were too large for reasonable means of transport. Even more so, while they are capable of running at any power, and can certainly be so set that the intensity will melt any structure, they cannot violently explode. The rapid rate of energy release is what makes an explosion. In the pile, the balance of neutrons made in the chain against those lost by non-fission capture is too narrow. The gain in number of fissions per generation is small, so that many generations are needed to produce a doubling of the intensity. Even more important, the chain operates on thermal neutrons. Such neutrons move at rifle-bullet speeds, and in travelling the many feet that are required to escape from the pile, they make a large number of collisions and eventually spend a lifetime of a thousandth of a second or so in each generation. Since many generations are needed, the time which would be required for the explosion of a pile may be measured in hundredths of a second. A block-buster explodes in the time it takes for a detonation wave, travelling some five thousand metres per second, to cross the mass. This time is perhaps one hundred microseconds.* The deliberate explosion of a pile would have the character not of a bomb, but perhaps of a steam boiler bursting.

All the criteria for a weapon are satisfied by a very different kind of chain reactor, the kind from which an atomic bomb is actually made. The reactor is not a large and carefully arranged lattice of moderator and natural uranium, but a small compact mass of nearly pure fissionable material. Instead of the tons of even the best pile, the critical mass of a sphere of pure plutonium or highly-enriched U235 is measured in kilograms. The loss of neutrons to

* Throughout this article we shall find it convenient to measure time in millionths of a second, or microseconds. A high-velocity rifle bullet could cross the letter 'o' in one microsecond.

the chain by non-fission capture is nearly zero, so that the reproduction factor is large, much greater than the near-unity value of the pile. Perhaps most important, the chain no longer operates on thermal neutrons. Even the primary fission neutrons have a good chance of producing daughters for the chain. Only a few collisions make up the whole life-history of even an unusually long-lived neutron, and the fast neutrons move not at rifle-bullet velocities, but at velocities many thousands of times greater. A typical fast neutron would travel from Los Alamos to London in a second. A generation in the small chain reactor which is a bomb, is measured by the time that it takes a fast neutron to travel a few inches. The time is perhaps a hundredth of a microsecond. And the intensity increases markedly in a single generation if we use a mass well above the critical mass.

How many generations are needed for an explosion? We know that the energy released from the fission of a pound of fissionable material is about that resulting from the explosion of eight thousand tons of TNT. The present atomic bomb, which yields the energy of some twenty thousand tons of TNT, must therefore consume a couple of pounds of material. If to every fissioned atom we assign one neutron – the one that did the job – we must have released two grams of neutrons at least in the explosion. But in two grams of neutrons there are about 10^{24} particles. All of these descend from a single neutron which initiates the chain. If we needed, for the sake of example, only one generation to double the intensity, this would mean about seventy-five generations of the complete chain. The whole process would take only a microsecond, and the violence of the true explosion would clearly be present. This is the very opposite of the controlled reaction of the pile. It is worth while noting that the delayed neutrons, which are not even emitted for tenths of seconds after fission, play no part whatever in the explosion of the bomb, though their role is determining in pile operation. The two applications of the nuclear chain are as different as the burning of coal and the detonation of TNT. It is not the least remarkable property of the fission chain that the same mechanism can act in two situations physically so different.

THE CHAIN STARTS. From all this it is perfectly clear how to make a bomb. You must bring together enough fissionable material to have more than a critical mass. The more you assemble together, the less the proportionate leakage of neutrons out of the mass, the greater the increase of neutron intensity per generation, and the more rapid the whole process. The trick, of course, is to make the initial assembly. For the geometrical conditions and the nature of the material alone determine the rate of change of the neutron or fission intensity, and hence the energy release. There is no switch to turn the chain reaction on or off. You must do this by modifying the shape. If you have, say, two pieces of material each weighing nine-tenths of the critical mass there will be no self-sustaining chain until you begin to bring the two pieces together. As they draw close the neutrons which once escaped out of the neighbouring surfaces of the two pieces now have some chance to take part in the chain, because they are captured and induce fissions in the other piece of material. Long before you had caused the two pieces to make contact, the total configuration would have become critical. As the pieces approached even closer the reproduction factor would steadily increase, and the neutron intensity, had a chain started, would grow at an ever-increasing rate. If your actions were slow, the energy released would have melted the pieces long before they had approached contact. Under these circumstances the energy released would not be that of thousands of tons of TNT, but simply that sufficient to melt or otherwise destroy the assembling mechanism. Obviously this will not do. The solution is clear: bring the pieces together rapidly. Assemble them by making one piece the projectile of a small cannon, the other its target, placed directly at the mouth of the cannon. But recall the time scale of the whole phenomenon. Only microseconds are required for a tremendous energy release. Even special artillery will not move our pieces more than a fraction of an inch in this time. It is clear that the movement needed must be of the order of the size of the masses assembled, certainly several inches. There is only one way out of this dilemma. Nothing will happen to our assembling device if the chain does not start until the pieces are assembled.

Let us try to follow in words the incredibly rapid events which make up the nuclear explosion, beginning with the role of chance and ending with the catastrophe that follows.

THE TOSS OF A COIN. All the spectacular effects of the atomic detonation are started by an event as purely chance in its nature as the toss of a coin or the flip of the ball in roulette: the presence of a single neutron. If the neutron appears, by sheer chance, before the assembly has reached the degree of supercriticality which its designers had hoped for, the bomb will fail, though all of its components function exactly as planned. For the first time, perhaps, a single atomic event, a necessarily uncontrolled circumstance, can measurably affect the world of men. Again, if no neutron appeared, though some were expected, the projectile might pass through the target, and the bomb parts fly apart again without detonation. Of course, some ingenious though simple device can be introduced to prevent the fiasco of failing to get started on the chain, the fiasco of post-detonation. Any neutron source – such as a beam of radium alpha-particles arranged to strike a beryllium foil when the position of target and projectile is the best possible one – which can be turned on at the right time, will make it very sure that a neutron is present, by emitting many of them in the time the projectile moves only a short distance. But nothing can save the bomb from *pre*-detonation except chance.

However he may be intrigued by the philosophic implications of the predetonation problem, the designer of the atomic 'gun' must face it realistically, which is to say quantitatively. While he cannot escape pure chance, he may estimate how likely is his failure. He will not worry if after he has finished his design he is willing to wager odds of 100 to 1 that his gun will explode. No military venture has a chance of success much greater than that, neutrons or not. Is this high reliability possible? Let us make a guess at the numbers, using only pre-war information, and not the precise data now available to the workers of the Manhattan District. You will remember that the critical mass of U235 is measured in kilograms. Such a mass – even if we are pessimistic and take Dr Smyth's upper limit of one hundred kilograms – will be only about six inches in diameter. The projectile and the target will each be of this size in a possible design. Now when these two active pieces are within say six inches of each other, the neutrons from each piece will find their way with considerable probability to the other. The assembly will be supercritical. If the chain begins, it will build up to a high enough number to destroy the whole device in a few microseconds, as we saw above. The stray neutrons must be kept down. How well must this be done? The projectile in a light naval gun moves six inches in a fraction of a thousandth of a second (a long time in our nuclear scale, some three hundred micro-seconds). During this time, we should have no neutrons, or at least none to start the chain. It is clear that not all neutrons will start the chain. Some will be absorbed in the steel structure of our gun, some may even produce a fission, but the neutrons from the fission fail to find the active material again to continue the chain. About the average neutron we can make the sure prediction that it will begin a divergent chain reaction in a supercritical mass; but about a single neutron we must quote only probabilities. But we will leave this out of account, so as to plan for the most difficult case. We shall assume that any neutron appearing in this crucial third of a millisecond can make the bomb fizzle out. We must then require that during that time the wager is a hundred to one against any neutron appearing. Since the neutrons may come at any time taken at random, this is about equivalent to saying that in thirty milliseconds on the average not more than one or two neutrons appear. Where will neutrons come from? The Smyth report lists the sources: (i) cosmic rays, (ii) nuclear reactions in light impurities in the heavy metal, in which the weak alpha rays of uranium may induce neutron emission (analogous to the familiar radium-beryllium neutron-producing reaction), (iii) the release of neutrons by the spontaneous fission of the uranium itself. Let us estimate these stray neutrons. Cosmic rays produce a neutron at the rate of a dozen or so per square foot per second. The impurities, it can be shown by simple calculation, cannot produce even this many if the metal is quite reasonably pure. The spontaneous fission rate is publicly known for normal uranium through work published in 1940 in the *Physical Review* (the chief American physics journal) by two Russian workers, who first observed this queer phenomenon and there described it. Just as uranium spontaneously disintegrates by alpha-particle emission, it spontaneously disintegrates, though very rarely, by fission, without any incoming neutron to cause the event. The rate of such disintegrations is very slow. For every uranium atom which dies by spontaneous fission, tens of millions die by the emission of an alpha particle. The Russian work of 1940 indicates that between five and fifty neutrons will be given off spontaneously by a kilogram of normal uranium in one second. This rare event – so slow and improbable that it would take uranium from ten to a hundred million times the age of the earth to decay by this process alone – is the controlling factor in our problem. We do not know how this rate varies from isotope to isotope; let us assume it is the same for U235 as for U238. Then spontaneous fission will produce some five thousand neutrons per second in our bomb, and is by far the chief source of stray neutrons. Our design cannot get the reliability we had hoped. Even if we take some advantage of the fact that every neutron will not start a chain, the chance of pre-detonation by a neutron appearing in the crucial three hundred microseconds is something like even, and not a hundred to one. We have been too pessimistic, of course. For some of the six inches of motion is near the fully assembled position and here the predetonation will make very little difference to the final energy release. The problem is after all one of continuous gradation from dud to great explosion, and we have spoken as though it were all or none. But our numbers, guesswork as they are, still show that the controlling factor in bomb design may very well be predetonation.

Against this danger there are few measures the designer can take. He can reduce the cosmic ray and impurity neutrons by shielding and by painstaking purification. But their importance is not great. He cannot affect the spontaneous fission rate. To reduce the probability of pre-detonation he may reduce the amount of material in the bomb. When he does this, of course, he reduces the potential energy release. He must use at least a reasonably supercritical total mass. The spontaneous fission rate of the particular isotope which is his active material will thus help determine the size of his bomb: it cannot be too small, or it will not be sufficiently supercritical, nor can it be too large, or the spontaneous fission may cause pre-detonation. Only one thing is at his choice. As the Smyth report says, he may 'reduce the time of assembly to a minimum'. He may shoot the two parts together at great speed. In this way he can cut the chance of a fizzle just in proportion to the amount by which he reduces the time of assembly. The atomic bomb is simple, but its design is not easy!

THE CHAIN IS UNDER WAY. Let us trace the explosion still further. By chance and design, let us get projectile fully meshed with target. A neutron initiates the chain reaction. For illustration (we do not know the real numbers) let us assume as we did before that a single neutron may be absorbed, and the resulting fission yields two to take its place. These two each give rise to two, and the chain is under way. In some seventy generations, one neutron has multiplied to a thousand million billion (10^{21}) and enough energy has been released to turn the materials of our bomb into vapour. This is still no nuclear explosion. Only an energy equivalent to that of some ten tons of TNT has been liberated. Everything now depends on the next generations.

If the reaction stops now, the atomic bomb is nothing but a costly and unreliable block buster. But if after seventy successful generations, only ten more can be sustained, the chain will yield the twenty-thousand-ton explosion which devastated Hiroshima. Time is indeed of the essence. As we have said before, the fast neutrons which carry the chain in the bomb require very little time to multiply. The whole of the first seventy generations can take place in about one microsecond, during which a bullet would travel hardly a tenth of an inch, or an explosion in TNT proceed a quarter of an inch further into the mass. And the next tenth of a microsecond will make all the difference between an atomic bomb and an ordinary one.

THE CHAIN REACTION STOPS. The nuclear properties of matter are not affected even under the conditions now existing within the bomb. The chain proceeds as usual. It will stop only by exhausting all the fissionable material – in a perfectly efficient bomb, this is the mechanism of the end of the reaction – or by some geometrical change which will alter the supercriticality of the assembly. If the now vaporized bomb expands, its surface will increase, and the chance for a neutron to leak out of the less dense active material into the outside world will grow. When sufficient expansion has taken place, when the chance for neutron leakage has so increased that the chain reaction no longer multiplies the number of neutrons present, the release of nuclear energy has stopped. The bomb reaction is ended. It is clear that if the bomb we have described expanded in all directions a foot or so, its density would have very much reduced. The chance that a neutron could escape from the mass without colliding with a fissionable atom on the way would have increased very much, and the excess of one neutron would probably no longer be enough to sustain the chain. To expand a foot in a tenth of a microsecond implies a motion at a speed of a few thousand miles per second, and an accelerating force corresponding to suddenly created pressures of millions of tons per square inch. It is as though the weight of ten battleships were suddenly brought to bear on every portion of a surface as big as a sixpence.

It is clear that some expansion will occur. This is in fact what limits the reaction. The details of the physics of this spectacular event will have to wait for later publication. Obviously the strength of solid materials plays no part in this phenomenon. All that matters is the behaviour of the intensely heated gases, their inertia, and the way in which the great blast wave can eat its way through the material of the bomb and the matter surrounding it, pushing out with these great pressures, until the whole device has expanded and the energy release has stopped. The release of energy in the form of the energy of motion of fission fragments, its transformation to heat, at temperatures beyond those of the centres of stars, and the expansion wave of the hot gas are all subjects of importance to the designer of bombs. For the key to the efficiency of a bomb is the speed at which this expansion takes place, compared to the speed at which the last few generations of the chain cause the energy release to multiply. The last tenth of a microsecond is the crisis of the end of the reaction, just as the first three hundred microseconds were the critical time for its initiation. The measure of the difference between nuclear explosive and ordinary cordite is found in this vast change in time scale. Nuclear explosions are fast.

The role of the so-called tamper, a heavy wall of matter placed around the active component of the bomb, is now clear. Such a wall will, of course, act as a cloudy neutron mirror: it will reflect back to the fissionable material some of the neutrons which might otherwise have been lost into space. This will make a given mass of material more super-critical than without the reflector. This is obviously a sought-for result. Even on the controlled piles such neutron reflectors are used. In the bomb they are less advantageous than at first glance appears, because the time that a neutron takes to wander into the tamper and come back to the bomb again will find it arriving long after its birth. By that time the neutrons present in the bomb have multiplied considerably in number, and the inheritance of reflected neutrons from an earlier and neutron-poorer epoch is no longer so important. On the other hand, a simple mechanical property of the tamper is now of great importance. The heavy tamper must be pushed out by the expansion of the heated active material. The blast wave must move into the tamper before expansion can end the reaction. The tamper really does 'tamp' the nuclear explosion, almost as the wooden tamping rod of the miner tamps the dynamite into the drill hole. It increases the pressure required for expansion, delays the final expansion, lengthens the time of the reaction, and hence increases the energy release.

THE EXPANSION: THE BALL OF FIRE AND THE MUSHROOM. In a fraction of a microsecond, then, the energy of the bomb has been released. From heat, part of it has become the mechanical energy of the out-rushing material of the tamper. Some fraction of the total is in the form of 'penetrating' radiation – neutrons and gammarays – which must be considered later. But just now the interest centres on the hot ionized star-stuff of the exploded bomb. Out the edge moves, until in a few score micro-seconds the whole mass occupies a sphere something like fifty feet in diameter. When the heavy uranium and steel bomb has been spread as thin as this, it no longer has the density of metal, but that of ordinary air. From this time on the expansion is slower, and the hot material mixes with the air around, by now also heated to an ionizing, beyond-white, heat. The air and the vapour of the bomb continue to mix and the heated mass eats further and further out into the undisturbed air, displacing and heating the layer beyond the edge of the hot sphere. When this hot gas has expanded until the pressure within is not greater than the pressure of the atmosphere it stops growing. Perhaps a millisecond has elapsed. The gas has formed the hot 'ball of fire' which measures many hundreds of feet in diameter and glows with a white heat for as much as a second or so. It is this hot ball sitting on the desert sand which turned it into the iron-containing friable green glass that carpeted the desert floor in the test explosion called Trinity.

The ball of fire then cools a little, by radiating away its heat. In a short time it begins to rise, like the hot air balloon that it is, and the cool currents rush in around it. It rises, leaving beneath it as it goes a trailing column of dust and cloud. The great column rises, carrying within it the active fission fragments left by the burned material of the bomb. It is incredibly radioactive. For the twenty-thousand-ton-equivalent bomb has within it about a kilogram of fission fragments. The disintegration of this radioactive debris in the first few seconds or minute of its rise represents the activity of a million tons of radium! The fission fragments, of course, are principally short-lived, and in a few hours or a day the far-spread activity has dropped by a very large factor. We who watched at Trinity could see the violet glow of heavily ionized air around the rising column as the material irradiated the upper air.

Everyone has seen the fantastic grandeur of the rising column of heated gases over the ruined cities. Two phenomena of special interest are seen in those fine photographs. The column itself is mainly a cloud, just like any thunderhead, except for the dust and vapour it holds, radioactive and generating heat. The cooler air of the upper air causes the water vapour brought up in the hot column from the air near the ground to condense and the cloud forms. As the column rises like the smoke from a chimney it may come to what is called an inversion by the meteorologists.

This is a layer of air warmer, instead of cooler, than the air below it. When such a layer is reached, the gas of the column will spread out and rise no longer. This is the formation of the mushroom. But some of the gas of the column is still being warmed by radioactivity. This gas is warm enough to break through the inversion layer, and the column sends another stem from the first mushroom cap. This too mushrooms, now very high in the air, perhaps six to eight miles. All of these grand and ironically beautiful phenomena can be seen in the moving pictures of the attacks on Hiroshima and Nagasaki.

THE SHOCK WAVE: HOW A CITY IS FLATTENED. We have left the ground for an account of the relatively lasting spectacle of the mushroom. But a grimmer and more important phenomenon has already taken place below. A large fraction of the energy of the explosion went into pushing aside with extraordinary speed a large mass of air as the ball of fire formed. The pressure wave which pushed aside the tamper as the bomb expanded continues through the ball of fire, and, leaving the ball of fire when the gases stop expanding rapidly, hammers against the undisturbed air with terrible force. This wave is called a shock wave. The physics of the shock wave, which differs only quantitatively in this atomic explosion from the similar wave produced by any explosion, is a subject once overlooked by physics in the main, but forged to a real completeness by the requirements of the war.

A shock wave is simply a sharp sound wave of very great intensity. In a sound wave the pressure increase, followed rapidly by an equivalent decrease, is small in magnitude. But the great compression which the push of the atomic explosion gives to the air not only increases its pressure by a very large factor, but also heats it, as a tyre is heated by rapid pumping. The sound wave so started travels faster than sound in the cool air still unreached by the shock. The shock front penetrates further and further. As it moves it represents a sharp boundary between two regions of air: one region ahead of the shock, yet untouched, still cool and at normal pressure; a second region, hot, compressed, just behind the front, where disturbances travel at high speed in the hot dense air. As the shock front moves it loses some energy by fulfilling its purpose, that is by pushing over anything in its path, but more and more its energy leaks away as heat, by conduction and radiation. The air in the very front of the atomic bomb shock is at first actually red-hot. The shock becomes increasingly less sharp; as it spreads in a great sphere the pressure excess and the temperature rapidly fall, and far away, the disturbance has faded out into an ordinary sound wave, and a rumble is the only evidence of its passage. All the phenomena of sound are associated with the shock wave: it may be reflected, it may leave shadows, it may diffract around obstacles. Such phenomena are responsible for the not quite predictable behaviour of a shock wave passing through the complex pattern of a city. All who have seen the results of an air raid incident will fully appreciate what I mean.

The wave itself is simply a transmission of pressure through the air, successive layers in turn feeling the compression. Behind the compression there follows generally a rarefaction, representing the wake of the original displacement. After the entire wave, both the increase and the decrease of pressure, there comes a real current of air, a wind, which may in such great explosions reach hurricane velocities near the centre, especially in constricted places like buildings.

How is damage done? The high pressures of the shock hammer on the surfaces of buildings. The air inside – ahead of the shock – is, of course, still at ordinary pressures. The difference in pressure represents a force which can break the strongest walls. Through every opening the pressure difference will force a current of air as well, a wind which devastates the interior of most structures lucky enough to withstand the main force of the shock. Here a few figures will make very clear what happens.

At about a thousand feet from the atomic explosion the excess pressure in the shock is as much as ten or fifteen times the normal pressure. This is the pressure needed to cause the death of a man from blast alone, from crushing the walls of the chest and smashing his ribs. At about twelve or fifteen hundred yards the over-pressure has dropped very much indeed. The excess is here only about a third of the normal pressure already present. This seems small, but it is enough to demolish most houses, brick, wood or stone. On an ordinary wall such a pressure difference means a thrust of fifty tons, the weight of a locomotive. Still further out the over-pressure drops more and more. At two miles, it is only a mere fifteen per cent of the normal pressure. But this is as much as the effect of a tornado, and will damage structures of any ordinary kind, and demolish the weaker ones. At three miles the effect is down to that of a strong gale, and only light roof tiles, signs, or such weak objects will suffer damage. In Hiroshima we found the first missing roof tiles and broken window panes at eight miles from the blast.

British readers will be impressed by comparable figures for the V-1 explosion: the killing over-pressure is there found only at fifty feet; the demolition pressure at seventy-five yards, and the tornado effects at two hundred yards. The explosions of the atomic bomb are by far the greatest man-made blasts ever observed.

One difference between the blast phenomena in the atomic

explosion and those of a block-buster is the duration of the over-pressure, that is, the depth of the strong shock front. The shock from a block-buster passes in a hundredth of a second or so: that from the atomic bomb will generally last many times longer, exerting its force against the structure walls for a longer time, and usually causing more severe damage.

The shock moves at first much faster than sound, but in a rather short distance comes down nearly to the speed of sound in normal air, about a thousand feet per second, or seven hundred and fifty miles an hour. Thus the two or three miles of Hiroshima which saw destruction from blast were flattened in the time it took the shock to cross that distance, perhaps ten or fifteen seconds.

THE HEAT OF THE BOMB. We lay on the ground nine miles from the tower in the desert where the first bomb was ready to detonate. The night was cold; the thin air of the high desert just before dawn made us shiver even though it was mid-July. Then came the blinding blue-white flash of the bomb and simultaneously the heat of the noon-day sun full on the face. That great heat out of the cold dawn at ten miles distance is for all of us who were at Base Camp the most deeply remembered experience. The bomb radiates a not negligible fraction of its total energy in infra-red, visible, and ultra-violet light. Its average temperature in the first second or so, when the ball of fire has opened up until there is a sizeable surface to radiate, is like that of the sun, or perhaps somewhat hotter. The effect at ten miles is that of many seconds of solar radiation delivered in a much shorter time. At one mile distance the radiation intensity is one hundred times greater than that we experienced. This terrible flash heat deeply burned most of the men and women in the street within about a mile from the explosion at Hiroshima. Many light cloth and wooden objects – curtains, mats – were set on fire. The flash was so short that no one could move during its main brilliance. As a result the shadow of the nose was sunburned into the skin of many present at the explosion in Hiroshima. We saw a horse with the shadow of a rail fence unburned on his flank, which was elsewhere raw and hairless. This radiant heat is after the blast the most important source of damage. Tens of thousands of dead and injured, and scores of secondary fires can be ascribed to the radiation of the bomb.

NUCLEAR EFFECTS: GAMMA RAYS, NEUTRONS, AND THE FISSION FRAGMENTS. For every uranium atom fissioned in the bomb, two fission fragments are produced. By the time the ball of fire has formed, these fragments are no longer screened by the dense matter of the bomb, but only by the dilute vapour of the bomb's debris. Thus the delayed neutrons they emit, and the gamma rays associated with the beta decay of the typical fission fragment, can freely irradiate the outside world.

About one neutron is produced by the fission fragments for every hundred fissions in the bomb. These neutrons spread out in all directions. They are however rather rapidly slowed down and finally absorbed by the nitrogen nuclei of the air, and do not reach any sizeable distance in great number. At Hiroshima Professor Nishina and his staff collected samples of every kind from the region below the bomb. Artificial radioactivity had been induced by neutron capture in many elements. In samples of phosphorus which they prepared from the bones of the many dead whose bodies were recovered within a kilometre of the blast the fifteen-day activity of phosphorus was especially strong. From such measurements they were able to estimate the number of fissions which had taken place. But the amount of neutrons reaching the ground from the height at which the bomb detonated was too small to induce any activity of more than laboratory significance. At the desert test, sodium activity in the salt of the desert floor was strongly excited. It is likely that few persons were injured by the neutrons emerging at Hiroshima or Nagasaki.

This is not true for the gamma rays. They too are emitted from the fission fragments into the air. We normally think of gamma rays as being very penetrating. Compared to the neutrons, this is true. But compared to visible light, gamma rays cannot pass through very thick layers of air. The energy of gammas is so much larger than the binding energies of electrons in atoms that every atom looks much like any other atom to a gamma ray. Ordinary light on the other hand finds air transparent, metal totally opaque. But to gamma rays air or earth offer the same barrier, weight for weight. Now, a thousand yards in air corresponds in mass to about one yard in water, or two feet in earth. Two feet of earth represent a rather heavy shield for gamma rays, and a few thousand yards, if you remember the added effect of the inverse square law as the distance increases, is a formidable shield, better than that installed at Hanford. Let us make a small computation. Suppose that two or three gamma rays are emitted for every one hundred fissions (as with delayed neutrons) in the seconds that it takes to produce the ball of fire. This represents more than 10^{23} gamma rays. At one kilometre, neglecting the effect of the absorption of the air, about 10^{12} gamma rays strike every square centimetre. The air shielding is small at this distance – perhaps as much as a factor of ten, but not more – and the actual irradiation would be about that which physicians estimate as a minimum lethal dose. Many persons at even larger distances in Hiroshima and Nagasaki died from gamma radiation. Three thousand yards further, however, the dose received would be down by a factor of nine from the inverse square effect of distance alone, and by about a thousand from the six feet of earth equivalent which the additional air represents. So at two miles distance there can be no noticeable effect of the gamma rays from the explosion.

Some of the fission fragments may be blown into the ground. At the test shot, Trinity, the bomb exploded only a hundred or so feet above the surface on a steel tower. The ball of fire containing the vaporized fission fragments rested on the desert sands. A portion of these active atoms became fixed in the glassy slag which was the imprint of the ball of fire. This material remained on the ground, and did not rise when the ball of fire drifted into the air. The region of the crater thus was made very radioactive. Early entry into this area was possible only in the lead-lined Sherman tanks which rumbled in the first two hours into the centre of the crater. The short-lived fission products gradually decayed. About a month after the explosion, the activity was down by a factor of hundreds from the activity observed when the tanks made their initial survey. A party of reporters toured the central region. But even then the ground was active, and no one would have liked to make camp at that blasted spot. The collecting of active samples of the green glass, which has become tacitly named 'trinitite', is still possible. The piece on my desk will still drive the counting dial of a Geiger-Muller detector set at staccato speed.

At Hiroshima and Nagasaki, the bomb was detonated high in the air. This was done both to enhance the energy of the shock wave, by taking advantage of a reflected shock from the surface of the ground, and to lessen the radioactive contamination of the earth. The ball of fire did not touch the ground. Very little of the fission fragments reached the ground, and no dangerous activity was observed at any time. No casualties were caused in these cities by early entry into the region of the explosion.

As the cloud and the mushroom drift across the country-side, the fission fragments they hold will in part condense out on to dust or water droplets, and the activity will gradually shower down on to the surface of the earth far below. The details of this phenomenon are strongly dependent on the weather: a hard rain through the active cloud in the first few hours would deluge the surface with dangerously active water. As time passes, the activity decreases and the cloud spreads; the danger from the contamination lessens. The direct gamma radiation is well shielded by the few miles of air between the surface and the cloud high above the inversion layers. Only if the atoms of the fragments are brought closer to the earth, as by actually falling upon it, is there any sizeable irradiation of the surface. About twenty or thirty miles from Trinity there is a mesa a couple of miles wide and ten miles long on to which a rather considerable activity fell. The New Mexico range cattle which were grazing there developed very noticeable loss of hair, greyness, and even ulcerated sores on their backs. It is dry in that country; the cattle received the dust from the cloud, and it remained for weeks on their backs, close to the skin, representing a serious though not fatal local dosage of radiation. The beta rays from the active material in contact with the hide of the animals much increased the effect.

A thousand miles away from Trinity, in Illinois, the corn-fields lay in the hot sun and strong rains of the Midwestern summer. The corn straw from certain of these fields is used for manufacturing the paper in which some sensitive photographic film is wrapped for sale. The batches of paper prepared from corn harvested a week or two after the test shot proved inacceptable to the film manufacturers;

it contained enough radioactive contamination to fog some of the film. A physicist testing some Geiger counters in Maryland, two thousand miles from the test shot, noted an inexplicable increase in the background activity of his instruments on July 19, which went away a few days later. Only when the news of the bomb over Japan was released did he see a reason, which he transmitted to the *Physical Review*. Local rains may have brought down some material from the dilute cloud passing over Maryland in the stratosphere winds. While there is no definite proof that either of these remote events were direct consequences of the first bomb explosion, their timing is most suggestive. It must be said that even more remote effects are not absurd. There are some 10^{24} active atoms of fission fragments produced in the explosion. Weeks afterwards, there are still 10^{18} atoms decaying per second. If these atoms had been uniformly mixed by the winds over a belt a hundred miles long, thousands of miles wide, and the full height of the atmosphere – which certainly overestimates the dilution – the resulting activity would still be conspicuous on an ordinary Geiger counter.

THE DEATH OF A CITY. In all that has gone before we have described the physics of the atomic bomb. But the bomb did not seem like an experiment in physics when we walked through the long half-ruined shed of the rail station at Hiroshima and saw the litters of the blackened wounded and dying. The bomb is a weapon: the most deadly and terrible weapon yet devised. Against any city in the world from New York and London to the hundreds of large towns like Hiroshima and Nagasaki, the bomb is a threat. In any of man's cities a strike from a single atomic bomb will claim some hundred thousand deaths and some square miles of blackened ruin. The shock wave will wreck brick as it does wood, the gamma rays will kill men with white skin as it does those who have a yellow pigment, the fire will burn the cotton clothing of Manchester manufacture as well as it did that of Kyoto. And the bombs, if they come again, will not come in ones or twos, but in hundreds or thousands. Their coming will wreck not cities, but whole nations.

Physicists have learned to say more than physics these days. I hope the reader will see the propriety of ending this partial account of the work of the great laboratory at Los Alamos with a few sentences from a speech of its wartime director, Robert Oppenheimer:

'. . . If atomic bombs are to be added as new weapons to the arsenals of a warring world, or to the arsenals of nations preparing for war, then the time will come when mankind will curse the names of Los Alamos and of Hiroshima.

'The peoples of this world must unite, or they will perish. This war, that has ravaged so much of the earth, has written these words. The atomic bomb has spelled them out for all men to understand. Other men have spoken them, in other times, of other wars, of other weapons. They have not prevailed. There are some, misled by a false sense of human history, who hold that they will not prevail to-day. It is not for us to believe that. By our works we are committed, committed to a world united, before this common peril, in law, and in humanity.'

Index